CASE STUDIES IN
CULTURAL ANTHROPOLOGY

GENERAL EDITORS
George and Louise Spindler
STANFORD UNIVERSITY

ABKHASIANS

The Long-Living People of the Caucasus

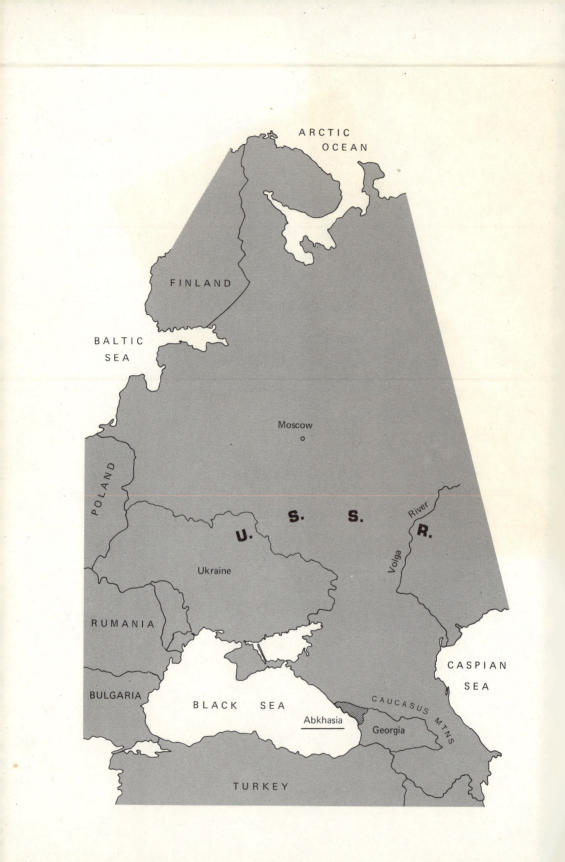

ARCTIC
OCEAN

FINLAND

BALTIC
SEA

POLAND

Moscow
○

U. S. S. R.

Ukraine

Volga River

RUMANIA

BULGARIA

BLACK   SEA

CASPIAN
SEA

CAUCASUS MTNS

Abkhasia

Georgia

TURKEY

ABKHASIANS

The Long-Living People
of the Caucasus

By

SULA BENET

Hunter College
City University of New York

HOLT, RINEHART AND WINSTON, INC.

NEW YORK   CHICAGO   SAN FRANCISCO   ATLANTA
DALLAS   MONTREAL   TORONTO   LONDON   SYDNEY

Cover photo: *An Abkhasian who has lived a century holds aloft his great-grandson, who has lived a year.*

Library of Congress Cataloging in Publication Data

Benet, Sula, 1903–
  Abkhasians: the long-living people of the Caucasus

  (Case studies in cultural anthropology)
  Bibliography: p. 111
  1. Abkhazians. I. Title. II. Series.
  DK34.A2B46   301.45'19'996   73–21655
ISBN: 0-03-088040-8

This book is dedicated to the memory of my parents.

Foreword

ABOUT THE SERIES

The case studies in cultural anthropology are designed to bring to students, in beginning and intermediate courses in the social sciences, insights into the richness and complexity of human life as it is lived in different ways and in different places. They are written by men and women who have lived in the societies they write about and who are professionally trained as observers and interpreters of human behavior. The authors are also teachers, and in writing their books they have kept the students who will read them foremost in their minds. It is our belief that when an understanding of ways of life very different from one's own is gained, abstractions and generalizations about social structure, cultural values, subsistence techniques, and the other universal categories of human social behavior become meaningful.

ABOUT THE AUTHOR

Sula Benet is Professor of Anthropology at Hunter College, City University of New York. She was born and educated in Warsaw, Poland, where she graduated from the University of Warsaw with a diploma in ethnography and archeology. She came to Columbia University for further studies on a scholarship and earned her Ph.D. in 1944 in anthropology. Her special field is Eastern Europe where she has done fieldwork over a number of years since 1945, under the auspices of Columbia University, the Social Science Research Council, the Research Institute for the Study of Man, and the Wenner-Gren Foundation for Anthropological Research. She is fluent in Russian, Polish, and Ukrainian. In addition to a number of articles in the field of ethnography, archeology, folklore, and drug use, her publications include the following books: *Hemp (hashish) in Folk Customs and Beliefs*; *Song, Dance and Customs of Peasant Poland*; *Riddles of Many Lands* (in collaboration with Carl Withers), a selection of the Junior Literary Guild; *American Riddle Book*, also with Carl Withers; *Festival Menus Round the World*; and *The Village Viriatino* (trans. and ed.).

In addition to Hunter College, she has also taught at Columbia University and Pratt Institute. She is a Fellow of the American Anthropological Association and a Fellow of the New York Academy of Sciences.

ABOUT THE BOOK

That this is the case study of a land and its people bordering on its southwestern perimeter the coast of the Black Sea, and that it is a part of the Soviet

Union, is cause enough in itself to make this study of particular interest. The Abkhasian Republic has a population only one quarter of which is native Abkhasian. The rest are immigrants including Armenians, Greeks, and Georgians. For this reason, too, the case study is placed in an interesting context, and one that is not atypical of the Soviet Union with its ethnic diversity and its recently mobile population.

Though the Abkhasian people are no longer in danger of extermination, they have fought for many centuries to maintain their independence against invasions from Persia, Arabia, and the Byzantine Empire, followed by the struggle to survive under Turkish rule. Even as late as 1866 the Abkhasians rose against the Tsarist government. Local Soviet administration was established in 1921, and many changes have been brought about since Soviet rule was established.

This case study, however, is not primarily about the relationships between the Abkhasians and the others who live in their country nor about the changes wrought by the Revolution and its aftermath of collectivization. The focus is upon the Abkhasian cultural system. Nothing about it has been published in English, and it is relatively unknown to students of anthropology outside of the Soviet Union. The study centers upon the village of Duripsh. Though there are regional and cultural variations within the native population of Abkhasia, we may regard this community as sufficiently representative of Abkhasian culture so that we may gain some insight into the whole. The case study includes a substantial section on kinship, including terminological, structural, and behavioral dimensions. Women's roles within the context of marriage and sexual behaviors, and child-rearing practices as related to the development of the individual character are described. A chapter on religion and folklore, together with observations within other sections, gives us some useful understanding of the Abkhasian world view.

What will probably seem most dramatic to many readers, however, is the fact that the Abkhasians are among what must indeed be the most long-lived people in the world. Recognizing their own unusual longevity, the Abkhasians formed a company of singers, dancers, and musicians consisting of thirty members. The minimal age requirement is that one be over ninety. These thirty were a small part of the over 2,000 persons age ninety or over in Abkhasia as reported in the official census of 1954. An astonishingly good state of health appears to be maintained by these people, who would be regarded as aged in any other culture. Persons one hundred twenty and older are reportedly in full possession of their faculties, put in a full day's work, and enjoy life. In her discussion of aging and the aged, Sula Benet makes it clear that these data are not based upon folktales but upon what appears to be good medical evidence.

With the longevity of the Abkhasians in mind, Sula Benet reports on the use of time, social behavior and roles, work habits, patterns of relaxation, and, of course, the diet and eating habits of the Abkhasians.

This case study is, therefore, not only about a relatively unknown people and their culture, but also about a way of life that apparently helps make it possible for an exceptionally large number of individuals to live to very advanced ages without the ravages that once caused General de Gaulle to say that old age is a dreadful illness, as he, a vigorous and long-lived individual, faced his final decline.

Old age and its trials or possible benefits is a subject of particular significance in the modern world, where increasing numbers of men and women live past their seventieth year only to find that they wish they had not, given the misery of weakness, illness and, perhaps worst of all, the experience of isolation from the rest of society, the awareness of being irrelevant, of being disregarded, that is the lot of so many older people, particularly in the United States.

The reader will find that many of the practices that Abkhasians follow as a part of their culture are indeed those that modern medicine would recommend if one wishes to attain a ripe old age in a state of relative health.

GEORGE AND LOUISE SPINDLER
General Editors

Landgut Burg
Federal Republic of Germany

Preface

For centuries, travelers have reported on the unusually long life and good health of the people of Abkhasia, an autonomous Soviet republic between the northeast shores of the Black Sea and the main range of the Caucasus Mountains. Today, the Abkhasians are attracting physicians, sociologists, and demographers, all seeking the magic key to the legendary longevity of this largely agrarian people.

As an anthropologist, I have been among the seekers; and while like the others, I have not found the magic key, I believe I have discovered some clues to the Abkhasian secret for long life.

I first went to Abkhasia in the summer of 1970 at the invitation of the Academy of Sciences of the USSR to do ethnographic fieldwork on modernization of their collective villages. Current anthropological research has been increasingly concerned with modernization in traditional societies, with the focus on agents of cultural change, such as peer groups, a modern administrative bureaucracy, an entrepreneurial elite, or institutions not indigenous to the traditional culture. Governments have generally viewed structures such as the nuclear or extended family, lineages, clans, and councils of elders as bastions of conservatism which must be weakened or destroyed if modernization is to take place. However, in Abkhasia, the kinship group was the primary institution through which successful modernization occurred. I believe this study will demonstrate the feasibility of using existing social structures such as the extended family as vehicles of cultural change.

While I was interviewing people who participated in the early efforts at collectivization in Abkhasia, and who still remember many events of that time, I became aware of the presence of unusually large numbers of people ranging in age from eighty to one hundred nineteen, who are still active in village life. Many of them are still working, though at a much reduced pace. The Abkhasians are famed throughout the Soviet Union for their longevity, and medical teams have been dispatched to study their diet and physical condition. It is my hypothesis that cultural factors, in addition to diet, exercise, and climatic conditions, bear some responsibility for the unusually long life and good health of the Abkhasians.

This work is the outcome of two years of research which started in 1971 and continued into 1973. During this period I have made three trips totaling eight months to the Soviet Union, where I was engaged primarily in fieldwork. The remaining time was used in an extensive study of published and unpublished reports by Soviet ethnographers, gerontologists, physicians, and historians. I conducted interviews in Russian, which all Abkhasians understand and which I speak fluently. I also used questionnaires. In addition, I was given the opportunity to examine extensive field notes, biographies, and genealogies collected by my Abkhasian colleagues, dealing with various aspects of Abkhasian life, past and present. They also helped by checking the proper translation and transliteration of Abkhasian terminology, as well as by interpreting folklore. I am deeply indebted to them for their generous help and friendship. My special gratitude goes to Dr. Yaroslava Smirnova of the Ethnographic Institute of the Academy of Sciences in Moscow, from whose many years of research in the Caucasus I benefited. I am also grateful to Professor Shalva Inal-Ipa, deputy director of the Institute of Abkhasian Language and Culture in Sukhumi and to Dr. Grigori Smyr of the same institute for help in collecting and evaluating my material. To Dr. Margaret Mead go my warmest thanks for helping me to untangle the intricate kinship patterns of the Abkhasians.

For great help in typing and editing the manuscript I am grateful to Martha Altman. My thanks go also to my cousin Eugenie Robinson, whose interest in my work and lengthy discussions have been a great source of stimulation. She also helped with the final typing and editing.

My trips to the Soviet Union were made possible by grants from the Faculty Research Award Program of the City University of New York, the Wenner-Gren Foundation, and The Social Science Research Council. I am grateful for their support.

Finally, I wish to thank the Abkhasian people for the gracious hospitality extended to me during my stay in their land.

Sula Benet

New York
December 1973

Contents

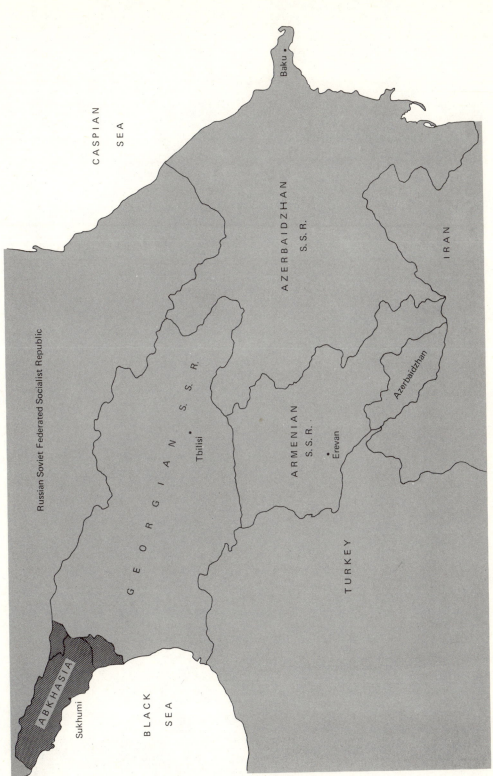

CASPIAN SEA

Baku

Russian Soviet Federated Socialist Republic

AZERBAIDZHAN S.S.R.

IRAN

GEORGIAN S. S. R.

Tbilisi

ARMENIAN S.S.R.

Erevan

Azerbaidzhan

TURKEY

ABKHASIA

Sukhumi

BLACK SEA

1/The Abkhasian world

THE LAND

Abkhasia is a hard land, and its people, expressing more pride than resentment, say it was one of God's afterthoughts. But it is also beautiful—a land of steep and thorny paths lined with primroses and orchids. Legend has it that God was distributing land to all the peoples of the earth, and when he was through, the Abkhasians finally arrived. However, they came late because they had been entertaining guests and it would have been highly improper for them to leave before them. God didn't want to send them away empty-handed, so he picked up some leftover stones and created Abkhasia. In spite of its hardships, the people loved their land.

You can cross Abkhasia in a day or two. The total land area is half that of New Jersey. To the north and east, the main range of the Caucasus Mountains forms the border of the Republic. This vast natural wall, averaging 9500 feet in height, protects Abkhasia from the bitter winds of the north. At the same time, the land is open to the warm, humid, southwestern breezes from the Black Sea. As a result, the climate is mild, with a mean temperature of 60.8°F–64.4°F. There is very little snow, though in 1910, a great snow fell—over two meters in depth, according to the old people. They still remember it as a recent event, and it has become a point of reference, along with the siege of Sevastopol.

The Caucasus Mountains are remarkably difficult to approach and ascend. They are crisscrossed by a maze of canyons whose steep walls are overgrown with lush foliage. Rapid streams descend from the perennial glacial cap of the main range of the Caucasus, emerging suddenly as waterfalls, collecting themselves in clear, icy lakes, and finally wandering down to the sea.

Though fish abound in these streams and lakes, they have never become a part of the Abkhasian diet, mostly because the Abkhasians have traditionally settled the higher slopes, avoiding the once swampy shores of the Black Sea and the constant risk of malaria. The swamps have since been drained, and malaria is now gone, but tradition persists, and fish is eaten only rarely. Fish is never served for any ritual meals and never to a guest.

The more temperate foothills are overgrown with oak, chestnut, boxwood, and yew trees. The underbrush is dense with ferns and thorn bushes, including a large variety of edible and medicinal berries. Until the development of modern methods

1

of agriculture, this rocky and thorny land impeded farming beyond a minimal supplement to herding and hunting; the hunter's task was not easy either. Even Abrskil, the Abkhasian Prometheus, complained about the thorns. The forest begins to encroach as soon as a field is left uncultivated.

In addition to trees and berries, many other useful plants grow wild such as persimmons which are used as a food and a cosmetic, pomegranates, and walnuts. At one time, thirty different varieties of grapes were cultivated, but now the type called *Isabella* is most popular.

The forest is inhabited by such predators as wolves, Caucasian foxes, jackals, otters, martens, weasels, wild boars, and bears, as well as great numbers of pheasants, turkeys, wild goats, and—on the almost inaccessible cliffs—deer. Swarms of wild bees produce an unusually sweet and aromatic honey which has been exported since ancient times, and for which Abkhasia is famous.

Up to 7000 feet above sea level, the dense virgin forest has a mixture of deciduous and coniferous trees. Above, one finds alpine pastures covered with lush grass and dotted with millions of flowers. These mountain meadows, and the crags above them, are home to herds of chamois (the European antelope), aurochs (a wild ox), and wild goats. Here too, Abkhasian shepherds bring their cattle, sheep, and goats each spring, moving their herds uphill as the weather grows warmer. Sections of the underbrush were cleared in the 1920s, after the Russian Revolution, in order to plant tea and tobacco and to pave roads, but most of the land remains overgrown.

Each homestead is at least half a mile from the next. For centuries, homesteads were selected for minimum visibility because Abkhasia suffered from raids and invasions. The home was built so that it could be taken apart and even the heaviest portions could be transported in a two-wheeled cart drawn by an ox or a donkey. But for the last couple of decades the villages have become more consolidated and the wattled huts have been replaced by two-story houses of wood or brick. Many of the old huts now are used for storage.

The southwestern border on the coast of the Black Sea is subtropical in climate, and the land bears palm, cactus, fig, and olive trees. Citrus fruits were introduced in modern times, and have become a profitable item in the collectively owned orchards and family plots as well.

Winter begins in December and is very mild. By late January and early February, roses, violets, and cyclamens are in bloom. The woods are green and scented with flowers by the beginning of April. The brilliant colors of orchids delight the eye at every turn. In the spring and summer people are busy with planting, sowing and reaping.

But autumn is the time Abkhasians love the most. This is the harvest time. The scent of ripened fruit fills the air. In September and October the trees are laden with apples, pears, oranges, and lemons, each branch heavier than the next. Every family has its own vineyard. In the autumn, large bunches of dark purple grapes are ready to harvest. People collect the grapes and tread them to produce wine in the time-honored manner. Birds also harvest them, eating so many that they sit stupefied on the branches, too heavy to fly.

THE PEOPLE

In 1970, the Republic had 487,000 inhabitants, nearly one-quarter of whom were native Abkhasians. The rest were Russians, Greeks, Georgians, Turks, and Armenians, who had settled after invasions and political changes. Never assimilated, these people live at peace with the tolerant Abkhasians.

Russians and other non-natives tend to cluster in the urban areas, whereas Abkhasians predominate in the villages. Even those Abkhasians who live and work in the cities still consider the village where their relatives live as home.

Most of the people in government are Abkhasian, as is the official language and life style throughout the region. There are only two cities: the capital, Sukhumi, with a population of 102,000; and Tkvarcheli, an industrial center. There are three urban spas, Gagra, Gudaut, and Ochamchir, and 575 villages.

Politically and economically, Abkhasia articulates with the Soviet Union. In the last forty years, the isolated semipastoral rural homesteads, producing at a subsistence level, have given way to a collective community whose income is based on cash crops of tea leaves and tobacco. In contrast to some other ethnic areas in the Soviet Union, where the shift to collectives produced a violent reaction on the part of the kulaks[1] and rich peasants, and consequent repression by the government, Abkhasia has made a comparatively smooth transition.

Little physical anthropology has been done in Abkhasia. The people appear to be related most closely to the West Georgians, and especially to the Mingrelians. They are mesocephalic, narrow-faced, and fair-skinned, with very dark hair and eyes. Redheads are rare, blonds even rarer. People's skin tends to wrinkle only in extreme age, with men developing wrinkles later than women. Graying of the hair also appears quite late, and baldness is rare. This, and their slenderness and erect posture cause the Abkhasians to appear taller and younger than they actually are. The ample figure is not appreciated. It is said that a man's waist should be so narrow as to permit a dog to pass beneath him when he is lying on his side. The Abkhasian has a distinct gait, walking with light, effortless steps. The old people maintain their unusually erect posture to an advanced age.

Both sexes are quite attractive according to Western standards. Old men develop bushy eyebrows which, together with their luxuriant mustaches, give them a dignified and even stern appearance. In the past, men often shaved their heads, but left beards and mustaches intact. The women are a bit shorter than the men, slender and graceful, with high foreheads, long thin necks, black eyes and long lashes. They have long, thick hair, which they braid. Older women pin up their hair in a heavy coil which they then cover with a kerchief. They greet visitors with shy smiles.

Generally speaking, the Abkhasians are modest in their dress compared to neighboring peoples such as the Georgians, who love ornamentation. At the present

---

[1] *Kulak* literally means fist. It refers to rich men of the peasant class who practiced usury and exploited poorer covillagers. When a poor peasant had no seeds to plant or not enough workers in his family to till his land, the kulak would rent the land from him, giving the owner a small amount of money or a small part of the harvest.

time, Abkhasians wear Western clothing, donning their national costumes only for holidays and family feasts.

A man's traditional costume consists of a plain cloth shirt with hand-made buttons, over which he wears the *cherkesska*, a garment common to all Caucasian peoples. This is a belted tunic with long sleeves, descending to mid-calf and bearing a row of cartridge pouches on the chest. Cherkesskas may be white, gray or black. An Abkhasian cherkesska is usually black. Several cap styles were popular in the 19th century, but all of these were replaced by the *bashlick*, a head-dress of soft brown or black cloth with two long ends hanging from either side of the head to well below the shoulders. The two free ends of the cloth may be adjusted to suit the wearer's needs. In the cold, the cloth is wrapped around the face, while in the summer the end pieces are tied together at the back of the head. Ordinarily, a man tucks his trousers into calfskin boots, but more elegant dancing boots are made of kid. The sole is cut smaller than the foot, and the boots are so tight that a man has to soak them in water and grease the insides before he can first put them on. As the boots dry, they assume the shape of his feet. However, the most important item of dress is a dagger in its silver filigree sheath. This, together with military decorations and a cane with a silver head, are the only traditional ornaments worn by Abkhasian men. Without weapons, the costume is unfinished and unmanly. In the past, when one could afford it, a revolver and a sword completed the outfit.

Men also wear a long felt cape called a *burka* to shelter them from heat and cold. When a shepherd or hunter has to sleep in the open fields, he wraps himself in his burka. In the past, women were not allowed to have burkas or overcoats—a custom intended to keep them close to home. Only old women could wear an overdress. At present, women wear Western coats and chiffon scarves.

Until the nineteenth century, the women's costume consisted of white pantaloons gathered at the ankles and a high-collared, long-sleeved coat of thin material, which flared out as it descended from the waist. From the age of eight or ten until her wedding night, a girl wears a narrow corset made of soft animal skin or strong linen. This serves to narrow the waist, flatten the breasts, and maintain an erect posture. Small breasts and a high forehead are considered most beautiful in a woman.

The Abkhasian language is incredibly difficult for a foreigner: it contains six vowels. Of the about eighty distinguishable phones noted, there are, depending on colloquial dialect or literary language, between fifty and fifty-six consonant phonemes, not counting the two semivowels classed with the vowels. There are five manner series of consonants: labialized, palatalized, glottalized, aspirated, and voiced in eight positions of articulation. Such a variety enables Abkhasians to become experts in the pronunciation of foreign languages as well as great mimics of animal noises, which aids them in hunting. The sounds cannot be represented exactly by any combination of letters in an Indo-European alphabet. The modified Russian Cyrillic alphabet currently in use is still not fully adequate to the task.

To an outsider, the speaker of Abkhasian seems to be producing a series of gentle explosions, although the vowels are expanded when people sing. The sounds include a wavering trill, whistling noises, and a prolonged buzz. The difficulty is compounded by the fact that the language is polysynthetic; that is, a complete synthesis of the predicate with the verb takes place. As one Armenian born and raised in Sukhumi said: "Who speaks Abkhasian? Only the Abkhasians do. The Russians gave up trying long ago." Even Caucasians speaking related tongues find Abkhasian unintelligible.

The people love their own language, which they consider beautiful and poetic. Much of the vocabulary preserves concrete images in the form of metaphor; for example, "helping leg" for staff, "mother's blood" for mother's brother. Onomatopoeic words are also common.

The verb predominates in an Abkhasian sentence. It can simultaneously incorporate two or more pronominal prefixes, in addition to prefixes designating the place, and some other affixes. Verbs express pronouns, numbers, grammatical classes, space, time, and other relationships with the help of prefixes, suffixes, and infixes. Without these modifiers, the verbs cannot function.

Linguists consider Abkhasian to be a branch of the northwest Caucasian group of languages, related to the most ancient tongues of the Near East, many of which are dead. They note that Abkhasian has shown remarkably little change over the centuries, in spite of frequent and intense contact with other cultures. Except for a few Arabic and Turkish words, there has been little borrowing. Russian words are used only to designate new technology and social institutions, and receive the prefix "a" to indicate that they are nouns. They remain Russian, however, and are not assimilated.

Before the Revolution, the Abkhasians had no written alphabet. Five successive attempts were made to give their language a written form. The first was an adaptation of Cyrillic script in 1922–1925. In 1925 the analytic alphabet was tried; in 1928 they tried working with Latin letters; and in 1938, another experiment was made with the Georgian alphabet. In 1954, the present alphabet was developed, based on the Russian but expanded to include fifty-eight letters (forty single and eighteen composite).

This new alphabet has ensured Abkhasian identity and cultural continuity. With its use, Abkhasian literature has blossomed: folklorists and ethnographers record the legends of the past; novelists, poets, and journalists write in their native tongues; and all their works are displayed proudly in the stores and purchased eagerly by the people. The creation of a viable alphabet, which allowed the written language to blossom, has also encouraged Abkhasian leaders to keep traditions alive, but to modify or eliminate certain extravagant customs.

HISTORY OF ABKHASIA

No one knows the origin of the Abkhasians. Nineteenth century writers thought them unrelated to any other tribe of the Caucacus. Their own legends indicate that they have always lived on the same territory, and that they descended either from a race of giants or dwarfs or both. All the evidence points to their continuous occupation of the land over the last three millennia. Some stories refer to early migrations from Asia Minor. Archeological, historical, and linguistic studies confirm the antiquity and striking continuity of their culture, despite centuries of raids and occupations by neighboring people. Invaders took slaves and cattle, but had no desire to settle on such poor land.

The Caucasian region has sometimes been considered a part of Asia, and sometimes part of Europe. For centuries, the inhabitants of this area have been mentioned in the chronicles of travelers amazed at their longevity and good health, as well as the multiplicity of tongues they speak. Ancient Arab writers called the Caucasus *Yubel-al-Suni*, "mountain of languages," and they were right. Over two hundred different ethnic groups live there, each with a distinct language.

Before the development of an Abkhasian alphabet, the only available history is a sketchy reconstruction based on ancient chronicles and records kept by outsiders. Toward the end of the first millennium B.C., the area was populated by many small tribes which underwent numerous changes of alliance, consolidation, and separation. These shifts eventually culminated in the formation of two confederations, the Abazins in the north and the Apsyls in the south. Today the people call themselves *Apsua*, preserving the name of Apsyl. Apsua simply means *the people*, or *the souls*.

During the sixth to fifth centuries B.C., two Greek colonies were established on the shores of the Black Sea for the purposes of trade and acquiring slaves. Subsequent Greek chronicles refer to the Abazgi. Pliny refers to Abkhasia as Apsies. The influence of this slaveholding culture quickened the development of commerce and may have stimulated the growth of social classes. Local tribes began to trade their produce—skins, wool, cattle, fish, bread, timber, wax, and honey—for weapons, fabrics and other manufactured goods.

Between the fourth and sixth centuries A.D., Abkhasia became a kingdom subject to West Georgia, itself a vassal of the Byzantine Empire. In 523 A.D., during the reign of Justinian, Christianity was declared the state religion, and was forcibly imposed on the people. Between the third and sixth centuries, the Southern Caucasian feudal system developed into a form which persisted until the abolition of serfdom in 1861 in Russia, and 1870 in Abkhasia. The feudal hierarchy was as follows:

Akh—prince of all Abkhasia
Atavad—prince-vassals
Aamsta—nobleman
Ashnakma—intermediate group between nobles and peasants; squires
Akhipsy—peasants with some obligations
Ankhayu—freehold peasants
Akhoyu—dependent peasants
Atey—slaves

This system was considerably modified by the traditional patriarchal clan structure. In the absence of a strong, centralized authority, with some noblemen not acknowledging the sovereignty of the ruling prince and some lesser nobles not acknowledging the dominion of greater nobles, lineage tended to carry greater power. Most political, economic and social functions were regulated by lineage.

The social order was based on two principles: (1) the right of each person to bear and use weapons and (2) family affiliations. Both sexes were trained in horseback riding and weaponry, and the right to use weapons distinguished a free person from a slave.

During the sixth through eighth centuries, the Abkhasian people fought for independence against Byzantine, Persian, and Arab invasions. These struggles helped to consolidate Abkhasia into a nation. Toward the end of the eighth century, Abkhasia and Western Georgia were unified under an Abkhasian king. The next two hundred years marked the highest development of local culture. However, feudal struggles in Georgia resulted in the incorporation of Abkhasia into a larger Georgian nation by the end of the tenth century.

Since the Abkhasians had no alphabet, some members of the nobility used the Georgian and Greek languages. Georgian became so popular that it eventually superseded Greek and a few families even took Georgian names. For example, the lineage of Shervashidze was originally called Chachba. Nonetheless, Abkhasian was cherished by the common people and remained in use along the Black Sea. The introduction of the alphabet has now precluded its disappearance.

The end of the fifteenth century brought the trying period of Turkish rule and the forcible introduction of the Sunni sect of Islam. The Turks also attempted to assimilate Abkhasians into their culture, and many individuals and whole families were enslaved and sold abroad.

From 1578, Abkhasia was under the protection of Turkey, but Turkey was not strong enough to prevent Abkhasia from having political alliances with Georgian principalities. During this period, Abkhasia was divided by the Georgians according to these established alliances. By the seventeenth century Abkhasia finally reconsolidated itself as a semi-independent state, but the people still suffered from the aggressive assimilation policies and increased slave-trading of the Turks. All these events impoverished the Abkhasian culture. Again and again the Abkhasians joined forces with the Georgians to fight the Turks, and finally in 1771 the Turks were driven out.

In the beginning of the nineteenth century, Abkhasia, together with Georgia and other Caucasian nations, sought the protection of the Russians, and in 1810 Abkhasia officially became part of the Russian Empire as a semi-independent state.

In 1864, when the Tzarist regime secured the Caucasus, Abkhasia became a province of Russia. But the colonial policies of Tzarist Russia did not suit the Abkhasians, and there were many peasant revolts—in 1821, 1824, and 1857. The largest revolt took place in 1866 in Lykhny, when a number of high Russian officials were killed by the Abkhasians. After putting down the revolt, the Russians confiscated all the weapons of the population, a measure unheard of in the Caucasus, and the Abkhasians were declared "unfaithful subjects."

Political and religious harassment from the Russians and misleading promises from Turkey, who wished to populate her barren lands with immigrants, led to mass emigration of Abkhasians to Turkey. Since large numbers of Abkhasians had already adopted Islam, they felt they had a better chance in an Islamic country than in a Christian one. Extensive migrations took place in 1858–1864, 1870, and 1877. Yet some did stay behind. In place of those who left came new settlers, loyal to the Russians, and Abkhasian land was turned over to them. Those Abkhasian Moslems who remained in their homeland, being unwilling to accept Christianity, were accused of disloyalty to Russia and to the Tzar.

At the beginning of the twentieth century, Abkhasia was a typical colonial province of Tzarist Russia. She was poor, underdeveloped, and over 92% illiterate in any language. In 1903 the people of Duripsh wrote a petition asking the government to make the two-class school in Gudaut into a high school, and to allocate funds for this. Of 150 people who were present at the meeting, only one could sign the document, and he did so with great difficulty.

Economically, Abkhasians in prerevolutionary times had lived at subsistence level with no industry and no working class. Some tobacco fields were planted around the turn of the twentieth century, but tobacco was not processed there. The few salaried workers earned very little. By this time, a kulak class was beginning to emerge from the originally egalitarian village, consisting of those peasants who held better and more land than their neighbors. Of course, the best land was in the hands of the local nobility. In 1909 the Tzarist governor of the Caucasus wrote that most peasants had to rent land and pay in crops. They had been reduced to sharecroppers.

Feudalism in Abkhasia, even during its highest development, was weak because of the mobility and independence of Abkhasians. Also, the peasants and princes were tied to each other by a network of ritual kinships which cut across class lines. They learned the same customs, had the same manners, and spoke with the same accent. If a prince were accused of a crime, he had to swear his innocence before the village assembly, just like any other man. By the time the Revolution came the nobility was so impoverished that they were on the same economic level as the peasantry and could not be considered enemies of the people to be stripped of their prestige and influence. Now, as in the past, the educated Abkhasian maintains close ties with his less-educated relatives.

Nevertheless, some class conflict existed, which was swept away by the Russian Revolution. In 1917 in the village of Lykhny, 3000 people—princes, minor nobility, and peasants—attended a meeting. The Akh, or prince of all Abkhasia, used to live in this village and a sacred tree several hundred years old grew in the square. At this meeting, the Bolshevik position predominated. Nestor Lakrba, a revolutionary leader, called for an end of the privileges of the nobility. When the nobles were ready to leave, the peasants were supposed to help them mount their horses, but Lakrba said not to do it. The nobles had to mount unassisted while the peasants stood by—a difficult thing, not because they were afraid, but because Abkhasians have a strong sense of obligation and propriety.

In 1921, Abkhasia became a Soviet Republic. In 1930 it became an autonomous part of Georgia and of the USSR. It is "national according to form and socialist in content." The new regime brought economic stability and prosperity to the Caucasus, an end to the perennial raids for cattle and slaves, and a tremendous reduction in family feuding.

2 / The long-living people

"Besides God, we also need the village elders."
ABKHASIAN PROVERB

A recent visitor to an Abkhasian family was being entertained at a feast, and following the local custom, raised a glass of wine to toast a man who looked no more than seventy. "May you live as long as Moses (one hundred twenty years)," the visitor said. The man was not pleased. He was one hundred nineteen.

The vigorous appearance of old people in Abkhasia makes it extremely difficult for outside observers to estimate their age. The lines on their faces and gray hair testify to their advanced years, but whether they are seventy or one hundred seven is almost impossible to judge.

The process of aging begins much later among the Abkhasians than among other people in the Soviet Union. Most of the aged work regularly. Almost all perform light tasks around the homestead, and quite a few work in the orchards and gardens, and care for domestic animals. Some even continue to chop wood and haul water. Close to 40 percent of the aged men (those above ninety) and 30 percent of aged women are reported to have good vision; that is, they do not need glasses for any sort of work, including reading or threading a needle. Between 40 and 50 percent have reasonably good hearing. Most have their own teeth. Their posture is unusually erect, even into advanced age. Many take walks of more than two miles a day and swim in the mountain streams.

The Abkhasian view of the aging process is clear from their vocabulary. They do not have a phrase for "old people"; those over one hundred are called "long-living people." One may call a person "elder," but this indicates relative position rather than age, although the two often coincide in Abkhasia.

Soviet gerontologists classify the later periods of life as follows:

60 to 75–"older"
75 to 90–"old"
Over 90–"very old," "long-lived"

Longevity in Abkhasia began to attract the attention of the medical profession in the Soviet Union in the mid-1930s. The first systematic investigation took place in 1930–1932 under the auspices of the Institute of Abkhasian Culture. A thorough and continuing study of the long-living people has been carried out there for many years by Soviet cardiologists, gerontologists, neurologists, and psychiatrists. More than fifteen medical doctors and other specialists participated in two expeditions, which conducted clinical and instrumental studies on forty people, ranging in age from ninety to one hundred forty-two, who were found to be functionally healthy.[1] This was the first time such a large number of aged people were investigated in the Soviet Union. In 1960–1961, research was conducted under the direction of the Institute of Gerontology of Abkhasia, studying 1395 persons aged eighty and over.[2] The most recent studies were done in 1962 and 1968, and reports were published in 1968 and 1970.[3,4]

According to the official census for 1954, there were 2144 people aged ninety and over in Abkhasia. As elsewhere, aged women predominated over men. Of the total population, 100,000 were ethnic Abkhasians living in the villages. Only 79 of the 2144 aged lived in urban areas. Of the ethnic Abkhasians 2.58 percent were over ninety. By way of comparison, for the entire USSR, 0.1 percent of the population had attained ninety years or more in the same year. There are no current figures for the total number of aged in Abkhasia; however, in the village of Dzhgerda, which I visited in 1971, there were 163 people between eighty-one and ninety, and 19 people over ninety-one, out of a population of 1200. That is to say, the aged in this particular village constituted 15 percent of the total, which is most unusual even for Abkhasia. It must be stressed here that this figure is not explained by urban migration, for young Abkhasians as a rule do not migrate to the cities.

Soviet demographers have calculated the ratio of people over sixty to those who have attained the age of ninety or more in different regions of the USSR. We will call this the "longevity quotient," L.Q., and express it as a percentage. According to 1970 data in Abkhasia, out of every hundred people over sixty years, 40.1 are over ninety. The L.Q. is therefore 40.1. In comparison, for the same year, the Lithuanian SSR had an L.Q. of 15.7. It means the Abkhasians have over two and a half times (2.55) as many people over sixty who have reached the age of ninety or more.

L.Q. can be interpreted as an index of the general health of older people in a given region (those in good health are likely to last longer). It is also a projection of life expectancy (having reached sixty, an Abkhasian may consider his chance of reaching ninety as 40.1 in a hundred.[5]

[1] I. Shafiro, Y. Darsania, I. Kortua, and V. Chikvatia, *Longevity in Abkhasia.* Sukhumi: Abkhasian State Publishers, 1956.

[2] G. N. Sichinava, N. N. Sachuk, and Sh. D. Gogokhiya, "On the Physical Condition of the Aged People of the Abkhasian SSR." *Soviet Medicine*, 5, 1964.

[3] Kakiashvili and Sadofiev, "Roentgenological Data on the Anatomy and the Function of the Circulatory System in Abkhasia," *Transactions of the Academy of Sciences of the Georgian SSR, 51*, No. 2, 1968.

[4] S. Rosen, N. Preobrajensky, S. Khechinashvili, I. Glazunov, N. Kipshidze, and H. V. Rosen, "Epidemiologic Hearing Studies in the USSR," *Archives of Otolaryngology, 91*:424–428, 1970.

[5] D. F. Chebotarov and N. N. Sachuk, "Long-Living People of the Soviet Union." Laboratory of Demography and Sanitary Statistic Institute of Gerontology, Kiev, 1972.

Considerable contrast in the health of the aged was also found in the Ukraine and Abkhasia. In the Ukraine, of the total population ninety years and over, those classified as functionally healthy constitute 32 percent for men and 20 percent for women; while in Abkhasia the proportion of healthy aged is considerably higher. It is 44 percent for men and 35 percent for women.

Drs. Kakiashvili and Sadofiev of the Georgian Academy of Sciences studied one hundred Abkhasians between the ages of eighty and one hundred five, in order to follow anatomical changes in the heart and major arteries. They concluded that "the circulatory system of the aged people of Abkhasia is characterized by moderate enlargement of the size of the heart." In another study, Dr. Kakiashvili found that changes in the lungs associated with aging take place much later among Abkhasians than among people of other cultures and climates in the USSR.[6]

In 1956, Dr. G. N. Sichinava of the Institute of Gerontology in Sukhumi, began a nine-year study of seventy-eight men and forty-five women over one hundred in Abkhasia. He reports their extraordinary psychological and neurological stability.[7] All were classified as "functionally healthy." Most of them had clear recollections of the distant past, but partially blurred recollection of more recent events. Some reversed this pattern, but quite a large number retained good memory for both the recent and distant past. The medical team verified events described by the subjects through documents and discussions with relatives.

All Dr. Sichinava's subjects correctly oriented themselves in time and place. All showed clear and logical thinking, and over 90 percent felt the need to do physical labor. Most of the aged correctly estimated their physical and mental capacities and showed a lively interest in their family's affairs, in the collective, and in social events. All were neat and clean about their person and physically agile.

Throughout the nine-year study, the majority of the participants seemed to remain unchanged in their personalities and reactions. Only seventeen showed edginess and some irritability over time.

E. J. Jachava, of the village of Gumista, was seen by the doctors over a long period of time. In 1938, at the age of one hundred, he was functionally healthy, very agile and fit to work. Sixteen years later, he was in the same condition. He was outgoing, good-natured, and talkative, and the only thing that annoyed him was that he could not hear well.

In 1958, at the age of one hundred twenty, he was diagnosed as having arteriosclerosis. In 1961, his behavior changed and he appeared somewhat timid and untrusting. In 1962, he was much less talkative and more passive. When the doctors proposed that he should be in the hospital, he agreed. As he was bidding good-bye to his family, he asked his daughter-in-law to serve food to the guests, which he should have done at the beginning of the visit. His daughter-in-law had no authority to serve refreshments without his orders. He was already ill, and died suddenly at the age of one hundred twenty-four.

Observation of the aged by other physicians confirms Sichinava's report of 1965.

[6] Kakiashvili and Sadofiev, 1968.
[7] G. N. Sichinava, "The Characteristics of the Nervous System and Psychological State of the Aged People of Abkhasia," *Anthology of Papers by Physicians of Ostroumov Republican Hospital in Sukhumi.* Sukhumi: Alashara, 1965, pp. 27–35.

In 1972, a team of physicians examined 3000 people aged eighty or more. The percentage of those classified as "functionally healthy" was 42.2; 36.4 percent were considered "weak," 12.4 percent "not well," and 10.2 percent required constant care. No psychological disturbances were observed in 79 percent of the examined population. Satisfactory vision was noted in 79.2 percent, and hearing in 88.8 percent. The overwhelming majority of those ninety years of age and over exhibited excellent mental health. The study of the protein-lipid metabolism showed insignificant arteriosclerotic changes. The respiratory system of the aged possessed "the greatest capacity" for compensation, and played an important role in adaptive reactions.[8]

Dr. I. N. Daraseliya studied the relationship between diet and coronary insufficiency among Abkhasian industrial and agricultural workers. The study group included 522 men between forty and fifty-nine years of age, among whom ten showed coronary insufficiency. Eight of these were industrial workers and two were collective farmers. Between the ages of forty and forty-nine, three industrial workers showed coronary insufficiency, and between fifty and fifty-nine, five industrial workers and two collective farmers showed coronary insufficiency. The medium level of blood cholesterol was higher in the industrial workers. On the average, the industrial workers consumed 24 percent more food, but only half as much vitamin C than the collective farmers.[9]

In an epidemiological study of blood pressure, Dr. Sichinava reported that he had observed over 127 persons aged one hundred years and over for a period of sixteen years. He found that over the years the aged showed no significant increase in arterial blood pressure. It remained within 110–140/60–90 mm Hg. Hypertension was found in only five persons, marked cerebral arteriosclerosis in six, and arteriosclerosis of coronary vessels in five.[10]

The extraordinary ability of the aged to recover from stress or illness has also been recorded on many occasions. One example is Akhutsa Kunach, one hundred fourteen years old. He lived with several generations of his family in the area where he was born. Dr. Walter McKain of the University of Connecticut and Dr. Sichinava visited him. During the previous winter, while cutting timber in the woods, he had been injured by a falling tree. Three ribs were broken. Two months later the doctors diagnosed him as fit to work, and he resumed all his former duties. He still felt responsible for his family, and directed the proper reception of his guests.[11]

Another example is Akhba Suleiman Klumovich, age ninety-nine, of the village of Achandara. He was interviewed by doctors in 1953. At the age of ninety-seven, in 1951, he had a bad case of pneumonia and became quite weak. It took him about two years to recover, and at the time of the interview, he claimed that his health was good, except for toothaches. The physicians examined his dentition and found that he still had 26 teeth. The hair on his head was gray and thick. He

[8] Sh. D. Gogokhiya and G. N. Sichinava, "The Older People of Abkhasia, their Health and Mode of Life," *Proceedings*, International Congress on Gerontology, Kiev, 1972.

[9] I. N. Daraseliya, "A Study of the Distribution of Coronary Arteriosclerosis and its Relation to Diet," *Anthology. . . .*

[10] G. N. Sichinava, "Long-Term Observations on Health of Long-Living People," *Proceedings. . . .*

[11] W. C. McKain, "Visit to a Russian Village," *The Courant Magazine*, April 16, 1967.

retained excellent sight and hearing. He had considerable muscular strength, and his face was unwrinkled. His cardiovascular system showed no pathology of any sort.

As is well known, the most characteristic pathology of the aged is disease of the cardiovascular system. The frequency of these diseases rapidly increases with age. They not infrequently result in disability and premature death. But in Abkhasia, signs of arteriosclerosis, when they occur at all, are found only in extreme old age.

American investigators who have done medical research in the USSR have substantiated Soviet reports about Abkhasia. A recent epidemiological study by a prominent ear surgeon, Dr. Samuel Rosen of the Mt. Sinai School of Medicine, was conducted together with Russian and Georgian colleagues in Abkhasia, Georgia, and Moscow. Dr. Rosen writes: "Abkhasia is one of the few places in the world with a high density of very old people, aged one hundred and over. . . . All the participants of our team were deeply impressed by their alertness, excellent muscle tone, and their mental and physical capabilities."[12]

The doctors did not find any cases of mental illness or cancer among the aged. Very old people do not succumb to heart attacks, but lose strength gradually, wither away in size, and finally die.

It would be a gross exaggeration to say that Abkhasians never get sick. Indeed, they do. The fact that they have discovered over five hundred medicinal plants among their flora and have been using them for centuries is proof that medicines were needed.

According to the local physicians, Abkhasian folk medicine is not only ancient, but quite elaborate and reputedly very effective. The indigenous plants which they use to cure a wide variety of ailments include:

ap'akua (Latin, *Ranunculi*; Russian, *liutik*)—a member of the buttercup family, used in the treatment of malaria and measles.
ashkardatz (Latin, *polygonaceae*)—a bright red plant of the buckwheat family, used as an anticoagulant and for treating colds. The Abkhasian name means mountain root.
akhurabgitz—the plantain. Its leaves are applied directly to wounds.
scopolia—a plant of the belladonna family. Its flowers are used as an antispasmodic, and its seeds as a laxative.
valeriana—a root used as a sedative.
asafoetida resin—a rank-smelling gum resin, sometimes known as Devil's Dung, extracted from a member of the carrot family and used as an antispasmodic.

During the smallpox epidemic of 1914, when vaccines were unavailable or unacceptable to the people in most of the Caucasus, Abkhasians used a home remedy, *chacha*. It is 160 proof vodka distilled from grape skins, mixed with crushed garlic.

The people are also expert in setting broken arms and legs. Centuries of climbing high mountains, hunting, and riding horses have given them both the need and the practice.

When an old person falls ill, folk medicine is immediately applied. This knowledge is widely diffused, especially among old people, who are the first to be called

---

[12] Rosen *et al.*, 1970.

TABLE 1   STATE OF HEALTH OF THE AGED

Physical Condition	Male 80–90	Male 90+	Fem. 80–90	Fem. 90+
Healthy	52.6	35.0	43.5	34.8
Report feeling strong, energetic	21.9	14.6	15.8	9.2
Mentally healthy	81.8	77.7	74.0	79.3
Outgoing	83.7	79.9	80.1	81.4
Good vision	39.6	36.9	24.7	32.6
Reasonably good hearing	48.1	45.0	40.8	47.6
Decrepit	4.9	8.7	15.5	18.2
Feel themselves to be weak and sick	6.4	9.0	7.9	11.7
Poor eyesight	4.6	3.4	2.5	3.9
Poor hearing	11.2	10.3	14.5	8.9

From G. N. Sichinava, N. N. Sachuk, and Sh. D. Gogokhiya, "On the Physical Condition of the Aged People of the Abkhasian ASSR," *Soviet Medicine*, 5, 1964.

for aid. When this fails, the doctor is called or the person is taken to the hospital. Everybody, including the patient, expects recovery after treatment is applied. One never hears the expression of the fatalistic view, "Well, what do you expect at that age?"

Sickness is not considered a normal or natural event even in very old age, and it has to be counteracted. Death in the Abkhasian view is not the logical end of life but something irrational and, when somebody does die, people are permitted to show their grief and allow their emotions to flow freely, even violently.

VERIFICATION OF AGES

In order to establish the age of people who had no civil birth certificates or other valid documents, Soviet medical teams have examined birth and marriage certificates from local mosques and Greek Orthodox churches where accurate records were kept. In the past, Abkhasians obtained these certificates in order to establish the legitimacy of their marriages. Since they had no written language of their own, the certificates were usually written in Turkish by the Muslim mullahs (religious teachers), or in Georgian or Russian by the priests. The Moslems customarily made notes of important events, such as births and marriages, in a volume of the Koran.

The Soviet medical teams took great care to cross-check records by interviewing the aged and their families, which often extended to three and four generations. Long-living people tend to remain in the area where they are born, to marry, and have large numbers of relatives who can be interviewed. Most of their children have accurate birth certificates.

Yanukian Minas, age one hundred fourteen in 1954, had no documents to prove his age. Through a family history and the biographies of 104 people who are directly related to him, it was determined that he was married in 1863. A year later he had a daughter, who was ninety years old at the time of the investigation. A second daughter was alive at the age of eighty and living in another village. Through discussions with all his relatives, his exact age was finally established.

The Abkhasians are especially conscious of lineage and their status within the lineage depends on their age relative to the other members. This factor is itself conducive to good memory. In the village where I did my fieldwork, I was able to examine the records of the collective farm, which include the ages of the workers when they first joined. In addition, the abundance of familiar names for such relatives as great-great-grandfather is an indication that sufficient members of fifth-generational families exist to require their use.

Dr. Walter C. McKain, a sociologist and gerontologist on the faculty of the University of Connecticut, recently spent 13 months in the USSR studying Soviet methodology as part of an American Soviet cultural exchange program. He reports that the census of 1959 was followed up by a thorough survey of 4000 persons eighty years and older. First, documentary evidence was sought to support their statements to demographers; second, a lengthy questionnaire was administered by local physicians. It included such questions as age when married, age when first child was born, age when the siege of Sevestapol occurred, and age when the Turks invaded his village. "If a respondent really knew his age, his answers would give a consistent picture. If he did not know his true age, major discrepancies would appear. Unless the respondents (often an illiterate or semiliterate peasant) were extremely agile with numbers, any deliberate attempt to mislead the interviewer would also show up here."[13]

The local physicians were provided with questionnaires and a 272-page book of specific instructions for the verification of ages. Dr. McKain became convinced of the accuracy and integrity of the reporting physicians.

There was the case, too, of the elderly gentleman who became incensed when his daughter upset his wedding plans by claiming he was one hundred eight, and not ninety-five as he had told his bride-to-be. My friend, Makhty Tarkil, one hundred four, with whom I spoke about the case, said the explanation was obvious in view of the impending marriage: "A man is a man until he is one hundred, you know what I mean. After that, well, he's getting old."[14]

WORK

Retirement is a status unknown in Abkhasian thinking. From the beginning of life until its end, an Abkhasian does what he is capable of doing. He and those around him consider work vital to life. He makes only those demands on himself that he can meet and as those demands diminish with age, his status in the community nevertheless increases.

In his nine-year study of aged Abkhasians, Dr. Sichinava made a detailed exami-

---

[13] Walter C. McKain, "Are They Really That Old? Some Observations concerning Extreme Old Age in the Soviet Union," *The Gerontologist,* 7, No. 1, 1971.
[14] McKain, 1971.

nation of their work habits.[15] One group included eighty-two men, most of whom were peasants who had been working from the age of eleven, and forty-five women who, from the age of adolescence, had worked in the home and had helped care for farm animals.

Sichinava found that the work load decreased considerably between the ages of eighty and ninety for forty-eight of the men, and between ninety and one hundred for the rest. Among the women, twenty-seven started doing less work between the ages of eighty and ninety, and the others slowed down after reaching ninety.

The few men who had been shepherds stopped following the flocks up to the mountain meadows in spring, and instead, after the age of ninety, began tending farm animals. But some continued to climb to the mountains in the summertime, considering it a vacation.

Those who had been farmers began to work less of their land; many stopped plowing and lifting heavy loads, but continued weeding (despite the bending involved) and doing other tasks.

Most of the women stopped helping in the fields and some began to do less housework. Instead of serving the entire family—an Abkhasian family extended through marriage may include forty or more people—they served only themselves and their children; they also fed the chickens and knitted.

Sichinava also observed twenty-one men and seven women over one hundred years old and found that, on the average, they worked a four-hour day on the collective farm—the men weeding and helping with the corn crop, and the women stringing and hanging tobacco leaves in drying sheds.

Under the collective system, members of the community are paid, in effect, in piecework rates for the work they do. Dr. Sichinava's group of villagers over one hundred maintained an hourly output that was not quite a fifth that of the norm for younger workers. They maintained their own pace, working evenly and without unnecessary motion, stopping on occasion to rest for five minutes or so. They never worked themselves into exhaustion, nor did they ever push themselves beyond their abilities.

By contrast, the younger men worked rapidly, but competitively and tensely. Competitiveness in work is not indigenous to Abkhasian culture, but is encouraged for the sake of increased production. Pictures of the best workers are posted in the offices of the village collectives. It is too soon to predict whether this seemingly fundamental change in work habits will affect Abkhasian longevity.

It is important to note that the aged worker does not feel discouraged by his limited capacity, nor is he ever expected to compete with younger members of the collective. Some of the older workers, however, manage to accumulate an astonishing number of eight-hour workdays during the year.

Abkhasian workers have their own heroes: Kelkiliana Khesa, a woman of one hundred nine in the village of Otapi, was paid for forty-nine workdays during one summer. Khfaf Lasuria, now age one hundred thirty-two, worked on the collective

[15] G. N. Sichinava, "On the Question of the Character and Range of Work Done by the Aged People of Abkhasia," *Anthology*. . . .

TABLE 2   PARTICIPATION OF AGED MEN AND WOMEN
IN WORK ON THE HOMESTEAD

Kind of Work	Male 80–89	Percent of Aged Studied Male 90+	Fem. 80–89	Fem. 90+
Varied tasks (light)	76.0	63.8	67.5	64.7
All kinds of work in home	19.8	8.1	2.9	2.8
Chop wood, haul water	2.8	7.4	5.6	3.6
Work in orchard and garden	11.3	12.7	3.1	4.5
Care of animals and fowl	3.0	6.7	7.6	7.3
Cookery	0.5	—	3.5	3.6
Washing clothes	—	—	3.3	2.8

Summarized from Sichinava, 1965.

farm until 1970. When she was over one hundred, she held the record as the fastest tea picker on the farm. She no longer works on the farm, but she still does not want to become sedentary so she spends her time traveling by bus to visit relatives in other villages.

Timir Tarba has just turned one hundred. A few years ago, he was honored as a "Hero of Labor" for his cultivation of corn. He still works in the mornings for a few hours collecting tea and spends some time cultivating his own homestead plot.

Seilach Butba was one hundred eleven in 1972. He helped his son build a house next to his in the village of Amara. Seilach shaves himself every day and washes in the cold mountain stream.

Osman Bzheniya of the village Lykhny became a member of the collective when he was one hundred years old. In 1959, he was one hundred twenty years old and was still a part-time worker in the collective. His birthday was marked in the newspaper *Soviet Abkhasia*.

Bozba Pash, a man of ninety-four, worked on the Otapi collective 155 days one year. Minosyan Grigorii of Aragich, often held up as an example to the young, worked 230 days in one year at the age of ninety. (Most Americans, with a two-week vacation and several holidays, work between 240 and 250 days a year, some of them less than eight hours long.)

Both the Soviet medical profession and the Abkhasians agree that their work

TABLE 3   WORKING HOURS AND OUTPUT OF THE AGED

	Weeding	Picking and Husking Corn	Stringing Tobacco Leaves
Number of Workers	14 men	7 men	7 women
Norm for 8-hr. day (young adult)	14,126 cu. ft.	882 lbs.	328 feet
Output of aged	2,649 cu. ft.	93 lbs.	32 feet
Hours worked by aged	4	3:34	4:14

Summarized from Sichinava, 1965.

A group of the long-living people of Abkhasia visiting Sukhumi. The woman with the cane and the cigarette is the famous Khfaf Lasuria, more than 130 years old, who smokes a pack of cigarettes a day and drinks some vodka before breakfast.

habits have a great deal to do with their longevity. The physicians say that the way Abkhasians work helps to maintain optimal conditions for the vital organs to function. The Abkhasians say, "Without rest, a man cannot work; without work, the rest does not give you any benefit."

That attitude, though it is not susceptible to medical measurements, may be as important as the work itself. It is part of a consistent life pattern. When they are children, they do what they are capable of doing, progressing from the easiest to the most strenuous tasks; and when they age, the curve descends, but is never broken. The aged are never seen sitting in chairs for long periods, passive, like vegetables. They do what they can, and the piecework system of the collective permits them to function at their own pace.

An Abkhasian does not, at any stage of his life, become sedentary. That, he will tell you, is bad for his well-being. The story is told of a young university couple who

Salma Gamsakhurdia, 101 years old, with her granddaughter, a member of a tea farm collective.

moved to the city of Sukhumi, where the husband took an important position. He brought his aged mother from her village to live with them in an apartment maintained by a maid. Almost immediately, the elderly woman began to fail. "I'm dying," she complained. A doctor was summoned and his prescription was simple —"Return her to her village." Back in her village, again working a full schedule, the woman revived and even today is fully active.

Mosna Lakrba, one hundred two years old, from the village of Duripsh, told the author: "You know, I listened to Lenin. Work is good. I would like to work too, but I actually don't feel strong enough although I am not sick. Now I am in command of the children of my family, but I would like to do more." She undoubtedly felt in command, and not as a babysitter, of the many children in her household, where the young mothers, her daughters-in-law, worked in the various branches of the collective.

The old are always active. "It is better to move without purpose than to sit still," they say. They always begin the day with easy tasks, gradually working up to the more difficult ones. Before breakfast, they walk through the homestead's courtyard and orchard, taking care of small tasks that come to their attention. They look for fences and equipment in need of repair and check on the family's animals. At breakfast, their early morning survey completed, they report what has to be done.

Until evening, the old spend their time in alternating work and rest. A man may pick up windfall apples, and then sit down on a bench, telling stories or making toys for his grandchildren or great-grandchildren. Or he may take a short nap, usually out of doors. In fact, the elderly, and particularly those who spent their youths as shepherds high in the mountains, prefer sleeping outside on the veranda at night also.

The elderly look after the orchards, pruning the fruit and nut trees, removing dead wood, and planting young trees. It is their favorite work. They have a great love for their native vegetation, and they often go deep into the woods searching out wild shoots that can be brought home as cuttings to start a new bush or tree.

Another chore largely attended to by the old is weeding the courtyard, a huge green belonging to the homestead, which serves as a center of activity for the kin group. Keeping it in shape requires considerable labor, yet one never sees a courtyard that is not tidy and well trimmed.

The Abkhasian worker any age has a great deal of responsibility for the conditions under which he works. As an agricultural worker, he and the other workers see both produce and profit, and their effort is directly reflected in the prosperity of their families and the collective.

As a worker ages, he becomes more responsible for decision-making. All Abkhasian villages have a "Soviet of the Long-Living," and a Council of Elders. The chairman of the collective presents them with complex questions about the economy of the collective and problems which they are facing, and usually, they come up with workable solutions to the problems. The chairman of the village of Dzhgerda says that the collective benefits greatly from the advice of its older members.

The Abkhasians do not set deadlines for themselves. They only feel a sense of urgency during actual emergencies, such as when a crop is threatened by a storm, or a house is on fire. They do not tell you when work is going to be completed, once it has begun. They work well, but are not particularly ambitious.

Nevertheless, during national emergencies in World War II, the Abkhasians worked in triple shifts, proving themselves heroic in defense work, in holding mountain passages, and on the front line in defense of the Soviet Union. At the age of ninety-one, A. B. Gegeneva of the village of Merkhuli was given a medal for his excellent work during World War II. In 1963, at the age of one hundred eight, he was still in good health and wore his medal proudly, along with headdress and dagger, as part of his formal attire.

FOOD AND DRINK

In all cultures, certain foods and methods of preparation are preferred, but rarely does this choice coincide so well with the precepts of modern nutrition as it does in the Caucasus. The people are convinced that their food is more delicious as well as more nourishing than any other. Even Abkhasian scientists of international fame, and high-ranking Party officials who have dined in the world's best restaurants, are eager to return to the fare of their native villages.

They have firm beliefs about which foods are healthful and which, though edible, should be left alone. They seem to have an understanding of the nutrient and medicinal values of the vegetation which grows on their land and which they know to the last blade of grass. Every child is taught the value of each plant, whether edible or medicinal.

As a rule, the Abkhasians are slim and seem to have no excess fat, especially the old people. However, they do not give the impression of frailty. Overeating is considered dangerous, and fat people are regarded as ill. When the aged see a youngster who is even a little overweight, they inquire about his health. "An

Contemporary agricultural worker with mechanized farming equipment.

Abkhasian cannot get fat," they say. "Can you imagine the ridiculous figure one would cut on horseback?" But to the dismay of the elders, the young eat much more than their fathers and grandfathers do. Light, muscular, and agile horseman are no longer needed as a first line of defense.

Before each meal, men and women wash their hands thoroughly, the eldest going first. Cleanliness is prescribed in Muslim law, but Abkhasians of all faiths observe it scrupulously. Their kitchens, clothing, and utensils are simple to the point of austerity, but whatever is in use is clean. Although insecticide is not used in the fields, any food which is eaten raw is washed gently beforehand.

The food is cut into small pieces and served in individual plates. Some dishes with cornmeal mush can be served directly on a well-scrubbed wooden table, and eaten with the fingers. No matter what the occasion, Abkhasians take small bites and chew slowly—a habit that stimulates the flow of ptyalin and maltase, insuring proper digestion. Food is prepared and eaten the same day and traditionally, there are no leftovers. Even the poor dispose of uneaten food by giving it to the animals, and no one would think of serving warmed-over food to a guest, even if it had been cooked only a few hours earlier. Though some young people, perhaps influenced by Western ideas, consider the practice wasteful, most Abkhasians shun day-old food as unhealthful.

The diet, like the rest of life, is stable. Dr. G. N. Sichinava studied food consumption and preferences of seventy-eight men and forty-five women of age one hundred or more. They were interviewed to determine if there had been any changes in diet over their lifetimes. In addition, a precise account was kept of the food intake of fifty-four of these people during a three-day period, and of six people over a thirty-day period.

The diet of these centenarians during the various stages of life showed few changes. None of them displayed any idiosyncratic preferences for food out of keeping with the general diet in Abkhasia. Fifty-nine of them had fasted for religious reasons, but none reported that they kept fasts at present. Only two had undergone a long period of famine. One man had been a prisoner of war of the Turks, and had had less than enough to eat for four years.

In Abkhasia diet does not seem to change significantly with an increase in wealth. Protein is consumed in moderation, fat used sparingly, and the carbohydrates are primarily *abista* (cornmeal mash), vegetables, fruit and honey. The daily consumption of protein is an estimated seventy-three grams per person; fat, about 47 grams; and carbohydrates, about 381 grams.

Historically, milk and vegetables made up 70 percent of the Abkhasian diet; at the present they make up 74 percent of it. Abkhasians also make a large variety of corn meal dishes by baking, frying and boiling.

Aged Abkhasians consume around 1900 calories a day, 500 less than the U.S. National Academy of Sciences recommends for males over fifty-five.

Refined sugar is not a part of the diet. Before retiring, people who wish to have something sweet may take a glass of water with honey. During the autumn harvest, grapes are pressed for their juice, and cornmeal is added to it. The mixture is boiled for a few minutes, allowed to cool, and eaten as a pudding. Or a string of nuts may be dipped into it and dried for dessert. Fruits are dried for the winter,

Men cooking abista in the traditional manner.

as are chestnuts. These are cooked in milk or water, or they may be roasted and accompanied by wine.

Abkhasians, young and old, drink one or two glasses of *matzoni* a day. This variety of fermented milk has been used among Caucasian people for many centuries and probably originated in this part of the world. Matzoni is made from the milk of various animals, such as cows, goats and sheep. It has nutritional and physiological value similar to other cultured milks.

Matzoni has low curd tension, which means the curd breaks up into extremely small particles which facilitates its digestion. The fermentation is usually started through the use of matzoni grains, which in appearance resemble small, spongy grains of rice. These masses consist of milk constituents and microorganisms—in particular, Bacillus caucasicum and Streptococcus A.

Matzoni can also be produced by adding a few spoonfuls of the previous batch to fresh milk, either skimmed or whole. Fresh cottage cheese without preservatives will work too.

In appearance and taste, matzoni is very much like buttermilk. It has a high food value and, according to Soviet physicians, therapeutic properties as well, especially in the case of intestinal disorders.

A sweet dish, often served as dessert, is prepared with cornmeal cooked in honey and water, and resembles a thick, honeyed gruel. The mixture is spread on a wooden board, cooled, and cut into sections, which may be stored. This is also a ritual dish served at wakes and on special occasions. Hunters and warriors used to take it with them on expeditions, in special wooden boxes.

Large quantities of fruit are eaten raw as they ripen. The rest is stored for the winter or dried and used as needed. Thus many fruits and vegetables are used all year round—either fresh, dried, stored, cooked, or pickled.

Actually fresh fruit is available seven or eight months of the year. One usually finds cherries and apples on the table in spring, and pears, plums, peaches, and figs throughout the summer. During the autumn months, grapes and persimmons are served as well as apples and pears, which grow wild in great abundance. Citrus fruits, introduced by the Russians, have become a major cash crop.

Wild pears are cooked into a thick syrup, with no additives, until it resembles jam. This syrup is then used like honey in cooking. Pear jam is also added to hot water and given to sick people to induce sweating which they believe is curative.

Blackberries and raspberries are eaten fresh but are also made into syrups in the winter for sick people. Pomegranates are grown and most often are cooked with meat.

Vegetables are served cooked or raw, but are most commonly pickled. A favorite dish eaten almost every day is baby lima beans, cooked slowly for hours, mashed and flavored with a sauce of onions, green peppers, coriander, garlic and pomegranate juice. With rare exceptions, vegetables are preferred raw or cooked in very small amounts of water. For memorial rituals lima beans are cooked with crushed walnuts.

Nuts are used in large quantities, grated or crushed for cooking, or eaten whole. Almonds, pecans, walnuts, beech nuts and hazelnuts are cultivated along the coast and in the foothills. Chestnut trees grow wild and profusely, as do many other small wild nut trees. The local population collects large supplies of chestnuts for the winter. They are stored in a special place in the household where they can dry well, and then are used through the winter as needed. A particularly tasty dish, made of chestnuts, is a great favorite of the people. The chestnuts are shelled and then cooked for a long time until they resemble a thick mash. After that assorted nuts such as almonds, pecans, beechnuts, or hazelnuts are added to the mash. The mixture is then served warm directly upon a wooden table top. A small dent is pressed into each serving of chestnut mash and a small amount of nut oil is poured into the depression.

Toward the end of World War II, nuts were exported from the Caucasus and the people did not have enough for their own needs. An elderly Armenian woman who lived in Sukhumi told me how she once stood in line because she had heard a shipment just arrived. She rushed to the store. "We can't cook without nuts, you know." In front of her stood an Abkhasian man with a sack. She said to him, "Would you mind letting me get in front of you because I have only my husband, and I need only three pounds and you need a whole sack?" He answered, "Of course, lady, please go ahead, and if you don't mind waiting for me I will carry them home for you."

Most of Abkhasian food in one way or another is flavored with nuts, never butter. They also serve nuts made in a special way along with vodka, as we would serve hors d'oeuvres.

Abkhasians eat many plants which grow wild in their region, such as the barberry (*Barberis vulgaris*). This they combine with damson plums and tomatoes for a delicious sauce.

Large quantities of garlic, both cooked and raw, are consumed daily, because Abkhasians like the taste and believe it has medicinal properties.

Soups are unknown. The Abkhasians eat relatively little meat—perhaps once or twice a week—and prefer chicken, beef, lamb, and kid. The meat is always freshly slaughtered and either broiled or boiled for a minimal amount of time or until the blood stops running freely. Chicken is cooked only until the meat turns white. Not surprisingly, the meat is tough in the mouth of a non-Abkhasian, but the most aged Abkhasians chew it without trouble.

When meat is boiled, the stock is discarded, since the elders consider it harmful to the constitution. Meat is roasted in open fires on spits and skewers—either wooden or metal. Pomegranate juice is used for basting, enhancing the aroma and adding a reddish color. Pork is served during the winter, and then only by some non-Moslem families. Though fish abound in the rivers and in the Black Sea, the people rarely eat it.

Not more than two or three eggs are eaten a week, and these are either boiled or fried. A popular dish consists of fresh cheese cut into small squares and boiled with milk to which cornmeal has been added.

Fat from meat and poultry is not used at all, and butter very seldom. When meat is served, even the smallest pieces of fat are removed, and the people show a great dislike for fatty dishes.

In general, foods are cooked without salt or spices, except for *adzhika*, a hot sauce made of red pepper, salt, dill, garlic, coriander, onions, nuts, damson plums, tomato, and beet greens. This mixture is carefully ground on a flat surface with a round stone. The product is aromatic and bitter, of a reddish-brown color. Old people eat less of this sauce than the young. It is the only item in the Abkhasian diet which is not considered healthful by Soviet medical authorities, and one local doctor is of the opinion that it is responsible for stomach complaints. But Abkhasians think that adzhika improves digestion by stimulating the secretion of gastric juices and that it also prevents obesity.

Abkhasia, together with the rest of Georgia, is the vineyard of the USSR. Every homestead, no matter how poor, has its own vineyard. The popular Isabella grapes seem to produce the best wine, and are well adapted to the local soil. During the harvest, which begins in September and may last until January, grapes are such an abundant and favorite food that a man may eat fifty kilograms in a single season.

Wine is called "life-giving," and some physicians are of the opinion that it prevents arteriosclerosis. The local product is a dry red wine, not fortified with sugar, and of low alcoholic content. Both the very young and the very old refrain from drinking large quantities, though everyone has some with dinner and supper. One is expected to know one's limits, since getting drunk is considered boorish. Drinking is done in sips, just as eating is done in small, nibbling bites.

Even at festive meals, the old people decline substantial dishes, saying, "It's too heavy before sleep." However, at a dinner which the author attended, a man of one hundred four ate less food than others, but chewed his meat so slowly that he finished at the same time everyone else did.

Although they are the main suppliers of tobacco for the Soviet Union, few Abkhasians smoke. They drink neither coffee nor tea, but prefer water and wine with meals. If possible, spring water is used, but well water is acceptable. People will go to great trouble to obtain spring water, the women and young girls usually carrying it in pitchers on their shoulders. Most villagers now have running water, but tap water is used only for cleaning.

Breakfast is served shortly after people arise, usually between seven and eight in the morning. The Abkhasians usually begin breakfast with a salad of green vegetables freshly picked from the garden. During the spring, it always consists of watercress, green onion, and radishes. In summer and autumn, tomatoes and cucumbers are most popular, while the winter salad consists of pickled cucumber and tomatoes, radishes, cabbage, and onions. Dill and coriander may be added, but no dressings are used. The salad is followed with a glass of matzoni. At all three meals, the people eat their "beloved abista," always freshly cooked and served warm with pieces of homemade goat cheese tucked into it.

Dinner, the most important meal of the day, is eaten in the early afternoon, between two and three. Supper is served before bedtime, and is rather light unless a guest is present. Then it becomes a banquet.

The old people do not like to eat anything heavy before retiring and may take only a glass of matzoni.

In comparison with Americans, Abkhasians eat very little. When they are hungry between meals, they eat fruit in season from their own gardens, or take a glass of matzoni.

Except for knives and the kettle in which some foods are boiled, metal is rarely used in cooking or serving. Milk is kept in wooden containers, and shepherds heat it by adding hot stones to wooden bowls of milk, producing a salty, mineral taste.

In Western cultures, it is the duty of the host to urge his guest to consume; but here, the host is obligated to see that the guest does not disgrace himself by becoming drunk. Abkhasians never eat or drink until they are stuffed, for such excessiveness is considered very unbecoming. From childhood on, one learns that in eating, as in all other aspects of Abkhasian life, moderation is valued above all other virtues.

Soviet medical authorities who have examined the Abkhasians and their diet feel it may well add years to their lives. Metchnikoff, the well-known Russian biologist, has suggested that the matzoni and pickled vegetables, and probably the wine, counteract toxic effects of the accumulated products of metabolism in the body and indirectly prevent the development of arteriosclerosis. The cholesterol level of centenarians averages ninety-eight, whereas the upper normal limit for middle-aged Americans is 250.

In 1970, Dr. Samuel Rosen and a team of Soviet doctors compared the hearing of Muscovites and Abkhasians, and concluded that the Abkhasian diet—very little saturated fat, a great deal of fruits and vegetables—accounted for their markedly better hearing.

At supper, everything is done to promote a relaxed mood. Young and old sing traditional tunes and play their two-stringed instruments known as *apkhartsa*.

To tell a sad story at the dining table is considered bad manners. A tale is told of a family in which someone had died just before the arrival of a guest. The room where the dead body lay was closed off, and the family went through the motions of hospitality. Only later did the guest learn that a body lay in the next

TABLE 4   COMPARISON OF FOOD INTAKE

	Abkhasian and Other Industrial Workers	Abkhasian Collective Farmers
Calories	2800–3000	2350
Vitamin C (mg)	70	140
Protein (gm)	98	65
Fat	26	18

From Daraseliya, 1965.

room. When he reproached his hosts for not letting him know, they said that they could not make him unhappy before or during the meal.

POSITION OF THE AGED

Age has always taken precedence over wealth and social position in Abkhasia. The elderly represent the virtues of which Abkhasians are most proud: stoicism, generosity, and courage. They are the keepers of a tradition which enabled Abkhasia to survive the countless invasions and persecution under the Tzars. The older generation led the extended families into collectivization of their economy. As it turned out, they prospered economically under the Soviets.

Abkhasians expect a long and useful life and look forward to old age with good reason. In a culture which so highly values continuity in its tradition, the old are indispensible. Abkhasian writing developed only under the Soviets, and many important events would have been forgotten if not for the long memory of the aged for whom the distant past is closer than the present.

The elders preside at important ceremonial occasions, they mediate disputes, and their experience with local ecology is invaluable, as is their knowledge of medicinal herbs. They are the opposite of burdens; they are highly valued resources.

The extraordinary feeling of elderly Abkhasians that they are needed is not artificial or self-protective. It is the natural expression, in old age, of a consistent outlook that begins in childhood. The upbringing of an Abkhasian child, in which parents and senior relatives participate, instills family participation, responsibility, and a deep-rooted sense of place and person.

Indeed, the Abkhasian—one day old or one hundred years old—is encompassed in family, possibly forty or fifty persons on one homestead, three or four generations of great-grandparents, grandparents, uncles and their wives, cousins, and, almost incidentally, parents.

Old people are treated with due respect but are not excluded from any activities in which they wish to take part. Unless they are feeble or very ill, they know what goes on in their homesteads and all news is shared with them. They eat and drink the same foods as younger members of their families, though in smaller portions; they work, but do less of it. Their days are active. Special consideration of their age is honorific and does not extend to daily activity.

Two men from the village of Dzherda, Maksuta and Achgi Amichba, carry the same surname and are therefore considered to be part of the same family. They are contemporaries, each being 100 years old and a member of the Council of Elders of his particular village.

Khfaf Lasuria, 132, is the oldest woman in the collective village of Kuitouli.

Singers, dancers, and musicians—all over ninety years of age in Sukhumi, Abkhasia with their conductor.

In former times, the respect for elders was even more pronounced than it is at present. When the father sat down on any chair or bench in the house; the son could not sit down on the same chair during the same day. The young people never sat down when elders were present. Even now, a young man remains standing in the presence of a very old man. At dinner, the old people sit at the head of the table, as befits the heads of households.

The opinion of the patriarchal household head often prevails in family decisions. His authority is not arbitrary and must be exercised in consonance with law and custom, but his predominance is unquestioned, and he does not feel challenged by changes in the society. The young people are not waiting for his death in order to achieve independence or to receive separate shares, since independence is not based on separation from the home. Young people move out when "the pot is not big enough to cook for everyone"; that is, they leave when physical circumstances dictate rather than out of a desire to escape, and they build a house next door.

At present, each village celebrates a holiday introduced by the Soviets—The Day of the Long-living People—in which all the elders parade in full dress, and the rest of the village gathers to do them homage.

After years of singing, dancing, and instrument playing for investigating doctors, the Abkhasians decided to form a troupe of performers, each of whom was required to be ninety years of age or older. The group had thirty members at the start and many of these were well over one hundred. The oldest was a woman of one hundred thirteen, Khfaf Lasuria from the village of Koitol. She was an excellent dancer; and in the summer of 1972 when she reached one hundred thirty-one years of age she still danced happily whenever asked. A man of one

Shach Chukbar, 120 years old, a singer of folk songs.

hundred twelve, by the name of Lukasharia, recently received a medal for his performance in the national dance competition.

The troupe performs regularly before audiences who delight in their agility and the quality of their work. The troupe's standards are quite high and no allowances are made for age.

3 / Life on the land

FEASTING WITH THE ABKHASIANS

It is said that the Abkhasians live to entertain guests, and probably this is not much of an exaggeration. Feasts are occasions for peace-making, establishing friendships, putting aside anger, and gaining good will. More than mere tradition, hospitality is the law of the land. Those who neglect this moral standard are severely criticized. A man could have all kinds of virtues but if he lacked hospitality and turned away a guest, the whole community would be up in arms.

A guest is said to bring seven blessings with him, taking one when he departs, and leaving six with the host. Abkhasian men embrace and kiss in greeting; the host makes a circular motion above his guest's head and says, "Let all the evil spirits who may be hovering around you come to me instead." Women greet female visitors by slightly pressing their shoulder against the visitors chest. If the guest is not offered these ceremonial greetings, he may turn around and leave immediately. Men and women extend greetings to one another when they are on horseback by standing in their stirrups.

Seating arrangements are taken as seriously as in diplomatic circles. The place of honor at a meal is the farthest from the door, except when the table is set in the courtyard. When a meal is to be served in the courtyard, the most important seats are those closest to the house. When people eat in an open field, those of highest rank sit closest to a tree. For want of a tree, a mountain, or a river, the direction of the sun or moon will substitute. If it is pitch dark, an Abkhasian will drive a staff into the ground and use it as a point of reference.

The Abkhasians dislike an unstructured situation. In daily life, as well as on special occasions, behavior is highly formalized and predictable. Respect is conveyed by a hierarchical order, according to sex, age and kin status.

Before and after the meal, hands are carefully washed in the courtyard. All eating is done with the fingers. The oldest male must be first to wash his hands. Everyone must stand and wait until he is finished before they can begin to wash.

A visitor to Abkhasian households soon learns to recognize the signs of a festive meal in preparation. First, a child is sent to the fields to announce to the family workers that guests have arrived. They finish quickly whatever work they are doing and return home. Since workers are paid on a piecework basis they are free to put off work until the next day.

Typical homestead—village of Duripsh. The smallest house is now used as a kitchen. The second is the home of the two brothers and their families. The big house is for guests only. The smallest house is called the big house because the head of the family, the old father, used to live there.

In the courtyard, the author (seated in the center) talks to 104-year-old Makhty Tarkil (at far left).

In the meantime, neighbors arrive to see whether anything is needed to entertain the guests and to join in the feast. Abkhasian feasts often require considerable efforts and large supplies of food to produce a substantial meal. The help of neighbors, who may also be relatives, is indispensible.

According to tradition, it is the neighbors' obligation, not just good will, to contribute food and work and, if necessary, money to the feast. The amount of contribution is in accordance to the degree of relationship and the sum an individual can afford. This form of help has a special name, *akutsatei*, which means, "that which is placed on top." Of course, nobody pays money for services.

A legend is told about a robin who was busy arranging her nest when a guest arrived unexpectedly. She had nothing to offer him, and in her anguish and shame, she cut her breast open. Blood gushed out of the wound and stained her feathers. Touched by her sense of honor and hospitality, God decreed that she should live, but have red feathers on her breast, so that people would honor her. Abkhasian children, who often raid birds' nests, do not touch the robin redbreast.

It is said that "he who respects you, respects your stomach, too." A freshly killed four-legged animal must be cooked for a guest, and perhaps served with the less honorable chicken. The meat is carefully dismembered without cutting through the bone, and is roasted on a spit, except for the head. This is boiled and then placed on the table with other meats, so that guests can see for themselves what animal was slaughtered or what blood "was spilled" in their honor. The bull or cow is most honorable, then the lamb, goat and calf. Each piece of meat has its place in a hierarchy, with the most respectable being the shoulder and the next being the rib on the rack. The mother's brother traditionally gets half the animal's head. The man who carves the meat gets information from the host about the guests, their social position and relationship in the family, so that he is able to distribute each cut of meat properly. This is the origin of the proverb, "Look at the person and then cut the meat."

There are no servants in an Abkhasian family. It is the task of the young people to wait on the table. They regard this task as a way of honoring the guests, not as servitude. Even if the young must cancel their plans to go to the movies in order to serve an unexpected visitor, they do so with pleasure. The ritual of a family dinner with each member fulfilling his or her traditional task is so essential to Abkhasian life that no one would willingly exclude himself.

When parents are not home, the children are expected to act in their stead and to entertain guests in the proper manner. Even a twelve-year-old boy should know the proper rituals for handwashing, seating arrangements, and toasting. The children, like the adults, love oratory and practice with each other. I heard Uerik, the four-year-old son of a friend of mine, raise his glass of watered wine to toast his slightly older sister, "And may you study well and get good marks."

When one asks the young folks why they don't mind rearranging their plans at a parent's request, they say, "Oh, it isn't convenient, but we do it out of respect for them." They never express resentment. It gradually became apparent to the author that they do not *feel* resentment. Their sense of family unity, instilled from earliest infancy, is stronger than peer group loyalty, and lasts longer. The difficulties of conveying such a feeling to members of a highly individualistic society with "a generation gap" such as ours are obvious.

The people eat slowly and with a great deal of decorum. The entire banquet lasts many hours but since Abkhasians prefer lukewarm food, no one minds. It is considered an insult to serve a guest food which is too cold or too hot.

No matter how much one might want to get out of an invitation to stay for dinner, one simply cannot do it without insulting the hosts, their families, their neighbors, and the entire village. When we visited and an invitation was extended, we naturally had to remain although we knew it would involve hours and hours of feasting and wine drinking. In the area of hospitality, the host who manages to keep his guests the longest and feed them to the utmost of his resources is the one who is most admired.

Custom dictates that immediately after sitting down, a *Tamada*, or host of the table, is selected. The Tamada is always a mature man. His duty is to see to it that the toasts are conducted in the proper order, and he is privileged to drink two glasses of wine to everyone else's one. Abkhasians are good listeners as well as good orators. Each person is toasted in turn to the evident delight of all present.

The toast is a traditional oral narrative praising virtues, real or imaginary, of each participant and it is usually very long. Abkhasians like flowery, ornate comparisons in their speeches. With great flourish and eloquence, each in turn must express how honored he feels to be called on to make a toast. He must describe the person to whom the toast is proposed, and then speak of himself, his dreams and hopes in a beautifully poetic way. When a person is toasted he is supposed to wait until everyone has finished drinking to his health before he empties his own glass.

When a person at the table must drive home after a visit and must not drink, he is nonetheless given a glass of wine which he touches to his lips at the appropriate moments. When the glasses are refilled, he also gives and receives toasts. No one is left out.

The Abkhasians drink a great deal of wine at their feasts because of all the ritual toasting. Nevertheless, drunkenness is scorned in Abkhasia, as is any excess, because it is considered a sign of weakness. A person who gets drunk repeatedly is no longer invited to feasts.

Although food is carefully prepared for a guest, the phrasing of an invitation is always, "Come and be our guest," never, "Come for dinner." The emphasis is on socializing, not on food for its own sake.

The guest in Abkhasia is sacred and respected. Etiquette states that a guest should not be asked bluntly what business brought him. Should he come without an invitation, he is automatically entitled to food, shelter, and protection. In former times, a guest was to be protected not only by his host but also by the entire community, no matter who was pursuing him or what he had done. An Abkhasian folk story is told about a small rabbit who was being chased by hunters and hid himself under the cloak of one of the old men attending a village meeting. The old man immediately pronounced the rabbit to be his guest and flatly refused to surrender him.

The host is also responsible for the safe conduct of his guests on the road back to his own home. Not so long ago, a host was severely criticized by the people of Duripsh because a guest was ambushed and killed after he left the house. People said the host should have seen to it that his guest safely reached his destination.

As a result of this tradition of hospitality, a guest may come at any time, day or night. The best and newest building in any homestead is the guest house, and it is usually equipped with a number of beds laid out with clean linen, ready to receive a visitor.

The number of guests, of course, depends on the personality of the host, as well as on his social and economic position. Nonetheless, it is very important to have the reputation of being hospitable.

When important guests depart, a host drinks half a glass of wine, and throws the rest of the wine against a nearby tree, or if he is indoors, against a whitewashed wall. The resulting stains are displayed with pride, in memory of the various guests who have honored the homestead.

The host also presents a gift to his guest so that his visit will always be remembered. Generosity is rated very highly and is a major source of prestige. "What you are loath to give your friend will do you no good," dictates an ancient Abkhasian proverb.

The obligation of the guest is to offer no obstacle to the host's performance of his duties, so as not to deprive him of the blessings and the glory. Konstantin Lomia, an Abkhasian poet, expresses this sense of hospitality:

APSNI[1]

Apsni, Apsni;
I was born to your pathways,
To cross your length with width
To the farthest reaches,
Is hardly an effort.
Then why are you so proud?
Perhaps because
You're a generous host
Welcoming guests
Everywhere, always . . .

MAKING A LIVING

Agriculture has been practiced for centuries in Abkhasia, but it has never played a major role in the economy because suitable land is scarce and the soil poor. However, the mountain meadows always have been excellent for grazing, allowing animal husbandry and dairy farming. Formerly, the only manufacturing was the home industries of spinning and weaving, and the production of weapons by village blacksmiths. Modern manufacturing techniques have replaced these small industries, and very few homespun articles are in use.

Before collectivization, Abkhasians attended to agricultural tasks which periodi-

[1] Apsni is the native name for the land which the Russians call Abkhasia. Poem translated by Sula Benet.

cally became urgent through a work cooperative called the *kiaraz*, or "self-help." Volunteer males able to work were members of the kiaraz. The men went out in a group and worked each member's field in turn, giving priority to the corn closest to ripening, or the field thickest with weeds.

Each chore had a special name and a special song. While working, the men divided themselves into two teams for choral singing, and they entertained themselves with a song appropriate to the activity. During rest breaks, they held foot races or marksmanship contests, and the winner was awarded a prize. As was the custom, the field owner provided food for the workers, and the skin of the goat which had served as lunch might be the trophy.

If the men of the kiaraz passed the farm of a widow, they would stop and work her field also. If one of the hosts did not have sufficient food for the group, the members brought their own fermented milk and fresh cheese. They also supplied their own tools. At times each member brought a different item; one contributed his plow, another his oxen. At the end of a work day, the men relaxed by singing and dancing long into the night.

Before the Revolution, the kiaraz functioned as a local militia, continually ready to resist invasions from neighboring tribes. Each man brought his weapons into the fields and placed them within easy reach while working. In times of warfare, each took his turn as a sentry while the others carried on with the work.

During the feudal period, the local nobility claimed help from the kiaraz on the bases of kinship, neighborliness, or some other bond of loyalty.

The men of the kiaraz were the most respected members of a community. They had a working knowledge of the traditional law of their people, and they sat in judgement as a court of law. They were empowered by the people to confiscate and distribute property, and even to pass the death sentence.

Prerevolutionary Abkhasian agriculture was confined to millet, corn, wheat, barley, grapes, tobacco, and hemp. Farmers operated almost entirely on a subsistence level. Millet was the most important crop, but by the end of the eighteenth century, corn predominated. Abista, the staple food, was first made of millet or wheat, but is now made exclusively of corn. Land was plentiful for the limited population, and the concept of land as property was not well developed. There was practically no buying and selling of land and, until about 1870, none of the questions of land distribution which plagued Tzarist Russia were considered in Abkhasia. Inal-Ipa says that "woods in Abkhasia constituted national property, according to documents of the later half of the nineteenth century. Members of all social classes had free use of it as well as of fruit and plants of the land. As trade developed, many lineages made agreements with the Turks for the export of palm wood."

Each community was free to use as much wood from the forests as it needed for the homes of its residents, but Abkhasians were forbidden to sell or carry building materials from one community to another. Each village had six people who were appointed specifically to enforce this customary law.

After 1917, the kiaraz played a very important role in support of the Bolsheviks. The peasants were persuaded to accept collectivism by comparing the kiaraz with the collective farm, which was quite similar. Primarily because they were used to

The whole family harvesting tea leaves in the village of Duripsh.

the kiaraz work structure, Abkhasian farmers made the transition to collectivism more easily than most peasants in the Soviet Union.

In a typical collective such as Duripsh, the farm implements, draught animals, livestock, seed, fodder, buildings, and land are collectively owned by all members. They work the common land together, and each individual shares the revenues in proportion to the work he has done. The collective farm is governed by a management board, which is elected at a general meeting of the farmers. The management board supervises the work of the chairman of the collective, who is also elected by the farmers.

Today, much of the economy of Abkhasia is based on the cash crops of tea and tobacco. In addition, the farmers grow citrus fruits, tung trees, figs, olives, eucalyptus, bamboo, boxwood, and redwood. Beekeeping has retained its age-old importance, and honey, the only natural sweetener in Abkhasia, is used in large quantities. Beans, walnuts, and apples are harvested, while grapes are eaten as well as used to make the light Abkhasian wine. Once taken up almost entirely by corn, the homestead garden is now used for more valuable produce such as cabbage, tomatoes, and citrus fruits.

Tea is relatively new in Abkhasia, having been developed only after collectivization. The gathering season for tea leaves lasts about five months, and during this time, practically all of the people work, including vacationing school children. Abkhasian women, who traditionally had never worked outside of their own homes, have proven to be extremely capable leaf gatherers. When tea was first introduced by the Soviet regime, tea harvesting was left to the women. As the crop assumed a greater importance in the economy of the village, entire families began to take part in the harvest. Now, wages are paid by the bushel, and many families have become quite prosperous through their labors on the tea crop. Tea has become so vital to the economy that it is now called the "Green Gold of Abkhasia."

The average annual cash income per family in the tea region is approximately 1352 rubles ($1800). All of the income goes into a common purse, to be spent as the family decides. Currently the farms are only slightly mechanized, though most collectives plan to buy more tea gathering machinery soon. And since all of the basic needs of the villagers are met through their own resources or through the collective, cash income primarily is used to purchase luxury items. Radios are

Village of Duripsh. A young woman holding a basket of tea leaves.

ubiquitous, television sets less frequent, and even less frequently watched. While cars, tractors, and helicopters delight the Abkhasians, an expert horseman and an excellent horse are still prized over a pilot and his plane.

A major prestige item for Abkhasians is a separate house for entertaining guests and visiting relatives. When a son builds a home, he builds it next to his family's house, and all share the large front lawn in common. Also, the son may still share expenses and possessions with his parents. In a large family with many children, the oldest daughter-in-law may try to exclude herself to some extent from the collective attitude so that she may keep a few personal belongings for her husband and her children in her own room.

According to law, each household is permitted the use of only half a hectare (1.2 acres) of land, but in practice, many families use more. Each household is allowed twenty-five animals, yet many exceed the limit. They raise sheep, goats, cows, chickens, ducks, and geese for themselves, as well as vegetables and fruit in their gardens. Since Abkhasia has a certain measure of autonomy, and most of the people in each village are relatives, the law is stretched a bit.

Although Abkhasians are growing steadily more dependent on the cash crops of tea and tobacco, animal husbandry and dairy farming are still viable sources of food and income. For thousands of years the people of this region subsisted by raising animals and hunting. Archaelogical findings indicate that as early as the sixth century B.C., wild bears, sheep, horses, and bulls had been domesticated. By the 3rd century B.C., Abkhasians were raising goats as well. Much later, around the seventeenth century, easy and inexpensive hog farming was developed for purposes of trade.

The major duty of Abkhasian herdsmen always has been the care of sheep and cattle. At one time, cattle constituted almost the entire wealth of the region and was used as money for payment of debts, taxes, and fines, and for retribution in blood feuds. Abkhasian cows and bulls, though small in size, are of fine stock. Together with goats and sheep, they continue to provide a variety of meats and dairy products for market and home consumption.

Raising cattle has not been simply a means of existence for Abkhasians; it has also been a way of life. In Abkhasia, a man's luck or success is still measured in terms of cattle. When a man expresses an idea first in a conversation with another man, who also got the same idea but did not express it, the second man will likely say, "You will get the cattle before I do." And the good luck wish, "May the cattle be waiting for you" is used as a daily greeting.

Still difficult and often hazardous, the work of an Abkhasian herdsman at one time was austere and very dangerous. High up in a mountain pasture, far away from kinfolk, he had to protect his herd from constant attack not only by wolves and other predatory animals, but also by the brutal raiding parties of neighboring tribes. The herdsman did not eat the animals under his care, so at the same time he had to hunt for his own food. Some families and communities joined together to hire a group of herdsmen to care for their animals. The group kept a twenty-four hour watch over the herds, organizing their duty into shifts and counting the animals every day.

During the summer, the herdsmen slept in the open, except for the older men who often had a tent. The elders were so highly regarded that a young man considered it impolite to sleep in the tent with an old man, even when invited. In larger groups, cooks and hunters accompanied the herdsmen to the pastures. Game meat was cooked for all in a large cauldron, while the skins and antlers went to the hunters for clothing and home decoration. As winter approached, the herds were brought down from the pastures to the foothills near the village where shelter and feed were provided. The cooking pots were stored in caves in the mountains, ready for next year's meals.

Today, the herds still move between pasture and foothills with the weather. In late spring, as the days get warmer, the herds are moved uphill. The hotter the day, the higher they are driven, until they reach the alpine pastures. Months later, as winter approaches, the herds gradually are worked down the mountainsides, finally wintering in the shelter of the foothills near the village. The herdsmen and animals live year by year with a gentle rhythm, slowly alternating between alpine pastures and the foot of the mountains, between the warmth of summer and the chill of winter.

The organization of herdsmen has not been radically changed by twentieth century collectivism. All of the animals which formerly were owned by individuals are now held in common by the collective. In the past, herdsmen elected their own leader, chief cook, and assistant cook; now the selection must be approaved by the chairman of the Village Collective. But the division of labor remains the same as it has been for centuries. Honesty and cooperation are expected of everyone by the chief herdsman, who has unlimited authority over the rest. The seniority system places the older men of wisdom and experience in higher positions of responsibility. And since herding always has been considered exclusively as man's work, a woman still is not allowed to set foot in the pasture lands.

Some aspects of the herdsman's life have been affected by modern technology. It is now common to find a veterinarian working directly with the herdsman in the mountains. Helicopters ferry herdsman back and forth to pasture, and deliver meat and dairy products to market. As with most everything, these changes have been easily assimilated into the age-old life style of the Abkhasians.

At one time, hunting was an important economic activity, providing meat for feasts as well as furs for sale and trade. Today, though of less importance, hunting still provides income for the collective. Formerly organized into guilds, the hunters now form "professional" unions which, like the herdsmen, have a hierarchy based on age and experience. As in the past, hunters occasionally bring their kills down from the mountains to their families or their relatives for special feasts. The most commonly hunted game animals are still marten and wild goat.

Most Abkhasians, at one time or another, go hunting. If a man discovers that he has no meat for an unexpected guest, and he can borrow none from his neighbors, he most likely will ride by horseback to the nearest herdsmen, who usually have a generous store of freshly killed game. Many of the herdsmen who were adults before the Revolution still go up into the mountains for a summer vacation, and some of them still hunt. One well-known example is Hassain Gikoz, aged one hundred nine, from the village of Bagmarini, who reads without glasses and has a reputation as a sharpshooter.

HORSEMANSHIP

Horseback riding in Abkhasia is an ancient art. Horses were used in warfare and actually were trained to fight fiercely. A horse took part in the fighting by biting the enemy and protecting the master, trying to drag the enemy down to the ground from his horse. Women as well as men fought on horseback. In the family, ownership of horses was determined both by the horses' temperament and the various needs of the members.

The Abkhasians have a great passion for horse racing. Horses are considered precious possessions and are used only for riding, never as draft animals. Horseback riding is a necessary part of education for both sexes. When a child is three or four, his father and senior relatives begin to teach him how to ride. By the time the child is seven or eight he is capable of riding a horse at full gallop and has mastered all sorts of equestrian skills.

Public entertainment always contains exhibits of horsemanship which the Abkhasians call "play." This requires extremely precise and controlled behavior. A rider may stand perfectly erect on a galloping horse or he may slide under the animal's belly to pick a dagger out of the earth with his teeth or picking up coins from the ground at a gallop. The most difficult and highly respected equestrian feat involves some preparation. First, a section of earth in the courtyard of a household is sprinkled with water so that the surface becomes slippery. Moving off a distance of about a hundred yards, the rider rushes towards the area as fast as his horse can gallop. At the exact instant that horse and rider enter the wet patch of earth, the horseman pulls back on the horse's reins. The horse rears up and glides across the wet area. Both horse and rider are perfectly balanced with one another, much to the delight of the spectators.

In the past, the love for horses was so great that the Abkhasians were known to resort to horse thievery. To steal a beautiful horse was an honorable or heroic act, but to steal a chicken was contemptuous. Owners of good horses sometimes kept them in their kitchen at night to prevent thievery, but even then they were stolen. The owner retrieved his horse by giving a banquet and inviting the thief as a guest. He would let it be known that he wanted to become relatives with the thief. Of course, many gifts, according to custom, had to be produced to show the guest's gratitude, and among them the horse would be restored to its owner.

Horses were used in stealing brides and in war, where a good horse meant the life of the owner. Horses meant power, prestige and wealth. Donkeys and mules were used for transportation.

Abkhasian clothing was always adapted to horseback riding. It was light, yet warm. It could not be clumsy because fighting was done on horseback. The womens' clothing also was adjusted to horseback riding. Women not only rode horses with great skill but they also often took part in raids or battles with enemies.

N. Derzhavin writes: "In Abkhasia quite often one can meet during the night a woman dressed in a cherkesska and with a man's headdress on her hair, galloping together with the best fighters on a fast horse. And if there is a necessity to ford

Village of Duripsh. Boys training for races in which they will take part.

a river, or to fling herself on the enemy with a dagger, it is done and is not considered unusual for an Abkhasian woman.[1]

At present, families often invest jointly in a good horse so that it can participate in races organized by the villages. Some collectives own stable horses and keep special trainers. The young as well as the very old participate in the races.

[1] N. Derzhavin, *AMOMPK*, 37, 1907, Part 1, p. 12.

An old man demonstrating his horsemanship.

Every village in Abkhasia holds horse races. Competition exists not only within a village but also between villages.

Prestige is not seen as accruing to one "winner," and there is no desire to eliminate other people from the competition. The Abkhasians view wealth and prestige as equally available to all, with a reasonable amount of effort.

THE ADMINISTRATIVE SYSTEM

In a typical collective such as Duripsh, the administration is divided into two closely cooperating councils: the *Village Soviet* and the *Village Collective*. The Village Soviet, whose members are elected by secret vote every two years, holds political power and enforces Soviet law. All personal documents, pertaining to birth, marriage, scholarships, cultural activities, youth councils, roads, and housing, either must come from this office or be endorsed by it. The Village Soviet sends representatives to the District Soviet, which in turn sends representatives to the Regional Soviet, and so on up to the Supreme Soviet in Moscow.

The village selects forty-four deputies to the Village Soviet. About one-third of these are women. In Duripsh in 1971, forty were Abkhasians, two were Georgians, one was Russian, and one was Abazin (Circassian). These deputies work in committees: Agricultural, Budget, Education, Cultural, Roads, Health, and Youth. Every two months, they are summoned to a meeting to give progress reports. From their midst a chairman and vice-chairman are elected. All members eighteen years of age and over have the right to vote. Twice a year, the chairman reports to the members on the state of the collective.

Parade of the horsemen of Duripsh. Young boys sit on their fathers' shoulders. Boys often take part in the races, as do elderly men. I was told that the best horseman in Duripsh was a twelve-year-old boy. Photo by G. Alpert, 1971.

The Village Collective, whose members are also elected, is supervised by the Village Soviet. As the active executive council for the planned economy, the Village Collective's functions include direct accounting to the Village Soviet for days worked and wages paid, taxation, and the purchase of machinery.

In Duripsh, elected officials tend to come from the largest families. As always, these families, tending to vote as a bloc, have the greatest influence in the community. The largest number of families in Duripsh are of the Gumba lineage, which accounts for 65 individual homesteads. According to the village register, each homestead has approximately five to six people. Thus, the Gumba lineage should have a minimum of 325 members. It is not surprising then that the most important position in the village administration, that of Party secretary, was filled by Mr. G. Gumba. The chairman was a member of the Tvanba family, a lineage with about 246 members.

The village of Duripsh and the collective of Duripsh coincide in territory. Usually individual homesteads are a great distance from one another, but smaller villages tend to merge in order to economize and to maximize profits.

The collective of Duripsh has 2945 members. There are 175 other villagers who work in government-operated institutions such as schools, the hospital, and nearby factories. There is also an agronomist, an electrician, and a few artisans. All these people are paid a salary rather than sharing in the collective.

The collective members are divided into sixteen work brigades, each with its own elected leader. This brigadier coordinates work schedules and task assignments, and is responsible for meeting the quota set by the collective. The brigades are subdivided further into work groups. The administration tries to organize the brigades territorially, so that people may live near their places of work.

Individual homesteads usually are headed by males, but a woman may be the head of a household, for the criterion is age. Most of the homesteads are joint family residences.

In addition to the Village Soviet and the Village Collective, there is also the Council of Elders. Every village in Abkhasia has such a council, whose members are elected and serve without pay. They are chosen from the most respected elders in the community.

In the past, all business concerning the administration of the village was decided at a town meeting attended by all adult males. This was held in the village square, next to a sacred tree. The old men, considered the most wise in administrative matters, sat down in front, and the younger men stood behind them.

At present, the Council of Elders acts somewhat like a people's court, considering such items as questions of morality and the arbitration of disputes with the purpose of averting feuds. Its most important function is the attempt to reconcile tradition with governmental directives, which often has been done most successfully.

The Council of Elders has no power to enforce its decisions. Rather, it expresses public opinion. At times they must recommend something with reluctance, for example, when the Village Soviet desires to change local funeral customs, or to reduce the number of guests at weddings and feasts in order to save money. But the Council of Elders is consulted often, and its decisions are respected. Abkhasians show extraordinary devotion to their national customs, in spite of pressure from

progressive political leaders. And many times these leaders are themselves products
of Abkhasian culture. After publicly condemning a custom, they often will "about
face" and join in the ceremonies themselves.

JUDICIAL SYSTEMS

At the present time, there are three legal systems in operation in Abkhasia.

Soviet Law is applied primarily in economic and political situations. Also,
important criminal cases are brought to the courts instead of being judged by the
families or communities, as was done in the past. Abkhasians have made an
excellent adjustment to Soviet Law, for the most part permitting a modern judicial
system to replace the blood feuds and village meetings as a method of settling
major disputes.

Shiriat, or the Islamic law, is observed by the Moslems and applies almost
exclusively to religious ritual. However, some of the family customs bear resem-
blance to traditions common to Moslems everywhere.

The *Adats*, Abkhasian customary laws, are observed and respected by all. They
are self-imposed, unwritten laws dealing with retribution, family regulation, and
interpersonal behavior. Some Adats are recognized by Soviet law.

The striking feature of Abkhasian familial and national life is its lack of
conflict over values and ethics. The people are law-abiding, with a great respect
for the Adats and the Shiriat, which they consider just and workable. The Adats
are the most important laws because they touch upon every aspect of life. They
show some Islamic influence, but are for the most part pre-Islamic and pre-
Christian. Relations between people are not left to individual inclination and
temperament, but are carefully refined according to the Adats, with specifica-
tions as to rights, obligations, and the amount of courtesy due another person. At
one time, even violent acts such as stealing brides or blood revenge were
approved of by the Adats under certain conditions.

In the past, the Adats and the Shiriat resolved most conflict. Though only elder
males were permitted to pass judgement, the village meetings were open to everyone, and the proceedings were comprehensible to all. There was no need for a
body of specialists who were required to master a highly specialized language. The
pre-Revolutionary heroes celebrated in Abkhasian folklore are not Robin Hoods,
outlaws who championed an oppressed class, nor Ghandian men of conscience who
openly disobeyed unjust laws. Rather, they are the defenders of the Abkhasian people
against foreign invaders.

Even today, an Abkhasian cannot say of an action, "It's my own business." His
actions affect his family and can bring vengeance down upon them. The past
pressures of poverty and war, and the threat of feuds, made it absolutely essential
for one to learn those interpersonal skills which promote unity. And today, there
are no empty threats or barroom brawls. A man fights in earnest, or not at all.

If a man thinks his wife is not sufficiently respectful to his family, he may
divorce her. She may divorce him if he mistreats her. If she is unfaithful, he may
cut off a piece of her nose and send her home to her relatives, but he must prove

his case in court before he can touch her. Whatever his rank in society, a man must give an account of his behavior. Since the people do not think of their laws as being especially harsh, mercy is not considered a virtue, and an Abkhasian who asks for it or gives it is deemed a weakling.

Since Abkhasia had no written language until after the Revolution, an agreement was not considered binding unless witnesses were present. Broken words, regardless of the circumstances, still are interpreted as insults and have grave consequences.

Enforcement of the laws is left to the elders of the lineage, the extended and the individual family. The more important the crime, the larger the circle of relatives who are affected. At present, the most severe punishment meted out to a transgressor is the taking away of his family name, reducing him to a nonentity. A person banished from his own family can find refuge with another family, according to the laws of hospitality, but he is still a nonperson. In the past, a family might have killed a transgressor. Today, the loss of family name and relatives is considered so severe that Abkhasians say, "Why kill him? He is dead already."

4 / Kinship

"He who has no relatives will embrace a fence post."
ABKHASIAN PROVERB

THE IMPORTANCE OF KINSHIP

The kinship structure in Abkhasia is an all-encompassing design for living. It regulates relationships between families, determines settlement patterns, marriage rules, the position of women and the nature of group solidarity. Throughout Abkhasian history, centralized authority was either nonexistent or ineffective. The kinship system was *the* institution which integrated Abkhasia into a nation. Each kin group took care of its members and acted as an autonomous political unit in its dealing with other kin groups. Today, the Abkhasians remain a kin-based egalitarian society composed of aggregates of blood relatives and ritual kinsmen.

In times of crisis, sickness, or death, all kinsmen are informed. Immediately they converge on the homestead of an afflicted relative, offering help, taking over necessary responsibilities and acting together with the family.

I first discovered the pervasiveness of kinship rules when my friend Omar, an Abkhasian who had accompanied me from Sukhumi to Duripsh, introduced me to a number of people he called his brothers and sisters. When I had met more than twenty "siblings", I asked, "How many brothers and sisters do you have?"

"In this village, thirty," he said. "Abkhasian reckoning is different from Russian. These people all carry my father's name."

I took his explanation less seriously than I should have. Later, when I expressed admiration for a recording of Abkhasian epic poetry I had heard in the home of one of Omar's "brothers," Omar, without another word, gave the record to me as a gift.

"Omar, it isn't yours," I said.

"Oh yes it is. This is the home of my brother," he explained. When I appealed to the "brother," he said, "Of course he can give it to you. He is my brother." To complicate matters further, I later found out that every woman who marries one of Omar's brothers gives Omar a new name, so that everywhere we went, my companion was addressed by a bewildering variety of names: Omar, Grisha, Zhora, Suleiman. . . .

49

Abkhasian society was, and continues to be, organized according to a precise and all-governing kinship structure. All men and women reckon their descent from both their father's and their mother's lineages. An individual recognizes both sets of relatives, but his rights and obligations are different toward each set. Abkhasian kinship terminology contains all the information necessary to decide how to treat a kinsman.

In addition to consanguineal and affinal relationships, there are also a variety of permanent ritual kinship institutions in Abkhasia. All blood and ritual relationships involve lifetime obligations, and ritual kinship is not established lightly. However, if a man has no living blood relatives, he is adopted into some family. To deprive, someone of his relatives, as might be done to one who offended the family name, is the worst punishment possible, the equivalent of a death sentence. While no alternative life styles are permitted, no one is left out, and this results in a deep sense of security.

During the period of constant warfare and blood feuds, it was most important to establish friendly relationships with families who were either neighbors or business associates. This was accomplished through the establishment of ritual relationships. Even today, these are considered so important that, during my visit, a Christian man was asked to be the godfather of a Moslem child. Finding it odd, I inquired, and was told, "Oh, it doesn't matter. We want to enlarge our circle of relatives."

By symbolic behavior and kinship terms, a man elevates his mother's relatives, but his family name, his inheritance, his home, and his work all derive from his father's kin. For example, his father's sister's son is called brother, but his maternal uncle's son is called by the same term as his maternal uncle. All the males directly descended from his mother's brother will be his "uncle" or *aenshcha*, taking precedence over males of corresponding generations on his father's side.

Since, with rare exceptions, age takes precedence over youth, all of these "uncles" are not treated exactly alike. A man and his mother's brother are actually the closest relatives, and this is the most important relationship in Abkhasian society, carrying with it mutual rights and obligations. The uncle defends the rights and interests of his nephew, arranges his marriage, and supports him if he becomes an orphan. He also takes an active part in arranging funerals, mourns for his sister's children, and if he himself dies, his body is washed by his nephew, as a duty. If the nephew dies first, the mother's brother is supposed to buy a suit of clothes for him, called the *anshan*. This is displayed on the nephew's bed for a month after his death.

The sister's son's duty is to honor and respect him, even if the uncle is much younger than he. Regardless of age, the mother's brother always has the first place in his sister's son's home, and his sister's son gives him the first toast, standing in his honor. In former times, it was the honorable duty of the sister's son to avenge his uncle. The folklore contains a legend about Abrskil, the Abkhasian Prometheus, who fought God and was punished for it by being locked in a cave and made to suffer endlessly. It was his maternal uncle who attempted to free him. The term for mother's brother, *aenshcha*, literally means "mother's blood."

For women, there is no corresponding relationship to that between the uncle and nephew. A woman's primary obligations, after marriage, are to her husband's family.

"My mother" used to be the form of address for every female who came from the family of one's mother, no matter how young she was. Since coming from the family means essentially having the same surname, any woman with the same surname as one's mother was called mother. Grisha's grandfather's mother was a Tzugba. The maiden name of the wife of Makhti's son is Tzugba. Even though she is younger than Grisha, she is called his "little grandmother."

Relatives of the maternal grandmother, who have neither the surname of the father nor that of the mother, are not quite as close—the incest prohibitions do not apply quite as strictly to them as they do to other relatives.

AZHVALA

The largest group of relatives is called the *azhvala*, which means "those who belong to the same root," or lineage. (See Figure 1.) Each azhvala claims that it is made up of descendants of a single ancestor, and all bear the same surname. Membership in a lineage is reckoned from the father, as indicated by the suffix *ba* or *pa*, meaning "son." Members of an azhvala have always occupied the same territory. For example, the old family of Gumba occupies thirty-five homesteads next to each other in the village of Duripsh. Although territorial unity was disrupted by resettlement and migration, the unity of the azhvala was not destroyed.

In the past, the azhvala had economic, religious, military and moral functions; indeed, it encompassed all secular and religious authority, in view of the weak or nonexistent central government. It took responsibility for orphaned children and widows and for punishing members who violated the law. Its members raised cattle cooperatively and bore mutual responsibility for offensive and defensive action. Although some functions have since been taken over by the state, the unity of the family is still expressed through the strict and all-pervading loyalties, family religious cults and exogamous rules. Every azhvala has its family shrine, which may be a mountain, a place in the woods, or a sacred tree. At those sacred places, the whole lineage comes together regularly, bringing their offerings along with prayers.

Just as the extended family cooks in huge pots, members of the lineage in their yearly meetings have a feast cooked in huge cauldrons, which are stored from year to year by old respected members of the lineage. In the past the cauldrons were used during the time of community work, holidays, weddings and funerals. During the exodus to Turkey in the middle of the nineteenth century, the huge cauldrons could not be carried along. They were stored in caves and some years later, when members of the lineage returned to their homeland, recovered.

The azhvala, up to the beginning of the twentieth century, was the basis of political power. Each azhvala promoted its own members for positions of power. Each family was very eager to have outstanding members within its midst. Even today, the families have an important impact on Abkhasian life and political decisions.

The azhvala is an egalitarian organization, resting upon absolute reciprocity of obligation among all members, with no exceptions. In the past, even the prince himself would have to clear himself of an accusation by swearing his innocence on a sacred object before the whole community. Literally, no man was above the customary law.

The azhvala is led by a council of the eldest males, who are heads of households. Under the leadership of the chief, the *aila aikhaba*, the council decides on the most important matters affecting the azhvala. Usually members decide these matters among themselves, but if the question is very serious, they invite other people living in the community to their deliberations. Each azhvala collects dues from the individual families in order to pay for the annual feast at which a bull is sacrificed. The meat is cooked and distributed to all participants.

Members of an azhvala may be scattered all over Abkhasia, and may not know each other, but their obligations to each other remain the same regardless of distance and personal likes or dislikes. For example, the azhvala is exogamous, as has been mentioned, and the incest taboo is so strong that there is a real revulsion at the thought of it. One man of my acquaintance, a Ph.D. candidate, was riding on a train, where he met a girl whom he liked well enough to ask for a date. When she gave her name, which happened to be his name also, he was terrified and apologized profusely, saying "Forgive me for intending to court a relative."

ABIPARA

The azhvalas are subdivided into a number of *abiparas*. Abipara literally means "sons of" or "descendants of one father." Some azhvalas have more abiparas than others. In the abipara, it is easier to trace the relationship, real or ritual, and the members feel more closely related than in the azhvala. All usually know one another personally. The abipara is responsible for the actions of its members, to a much greater extent than is the azhvala.

My Abkhasian assistant belonged to an azhvala which contains seven abiparas; and his own abipara counts two hundred members. Each Abkhasian male or female knows exactly to which azhvala and abipara he belongs. Members visit each other's homes during holidays, come to each other's funerals, weddings, etc., and each family contributes ten rubles annually to the abipara's purse. The abipara meets regularly to take stock of the life of its members, praise some, censure others, give contributions to the needy, consider praises and insults suffered by members of the family in order to take action. When a member of an abipara is insulted, all members are insulted. When a member of an abipara commits a crime against law or tradition (actually, tradition is law), it is the abipara that first judges and punishes him for bringing shame on the rest of the family.

The most intimate and sacred tie in Abkhasian society is between the mother's brother and his nieces and nephews. As an example of the power and influence of this relationship, a man will greet the son of a woman from his own village who has married into another community in the following manner: "How are you, our son, our nephew?"—as if the man was the mother's brother, when in fact, he was merely a former covillager.

Young members of an abipara consider each other as brothers and sisters. As members of the same azhvala, they call each other *aeshcha*[1] (brother, or man who carries my family name) or *aekhushcha* (sister, or woman who carries my family name). If the parent of a young member dies, the young people of his age group mourn with him as though the deceased were the parent of all of them.

Kinship ties are reflected in language. The terms "our wife," and "our wives" refer to all the women of one's family, including the extended family or even the lineage. "Our children" refers to children of the same family name and "our son-in-law" is the same thing. The "sons of our sisters" refers to all the sons in the female line.

When a woman marries into an abipara, all the older folk refer to her as "our daughter-in-law." In former times, the young bride had to sew clothing for other members of the abipara, as well as for her husband's immediate family, if there were no young women in the other families. They would bring her the work, and she was expected to do it without compensation.

The land possessed by an abipara is known as *akyta*. Sometimes a whole village consists of one abipara. Any hunter coming home with a decent kill is expected to stop by the homes of the other members, and even if it were only symbolically, to share his kill with them. When a member dies without leaving sons behind, his inheritance is divided among the heads of the families of his abipara. They, in turn, are obliged to provide sustenance for his widow and marry off his daughters. The wife and daughters do not inherit. However, a father's untimely death does not mean that his widow and children are going to be treated as "poor relations"; on the contrary, they are treated as well as anyone else and sometimes better, out of kindness.

Each abipara, like the azhvala, has its own council of the eldest and its chief as well. It also has its collective holy days, forbidden days, and separate burial grounds. A member of an abipara must observe both the forbidden days of his azhvala and his abipara, whether or not they coincide. These are days on which certain types of work are prohibited, such as the hunting of a particular animal connected with a mythological event, sewing clothes, or lending certain implements. However, all other work continues.

Sometimes the forbidden days extend to three or four days in the week. A satirical story is told by the Abkhasians about a woman who had three forbidden days to observe because they were her family days, and three other forbidden days which were her husband's family days. She had only one day left to work. Once, when she and her husband were crossing a narrow and rickety bridge over a swift river, she prayed: "Oh! dear God, if I can cross safely, I promise that the seventh day will also be a forbidden day." On hearing this, the husband, who was walking behind her, pushed her into the river.

[1] Not to be confused with *aenshcha*, uncle, which combines *aeshcha*, "my brother" or "my blood," with *an*, "mother."

A-INDU

The term *a-indu* means "large house," and refers to the extended family. It has been recorded that during the last quarter of the nineteenth century, there were families numbering more than 100 individuals living in one homestead of twelve to fifteen huts. This kind of family can be traced to one progenitor: a father and his sons and their families, and so on. At the present time, the large house refers to the house where the parents live. As sons separated from the parents, they built adjoining huts. In recent times, these have been replaced by larger and better equipped homes. Yet the parents' house is still called the "big house," even though it may be the smallest in size.

The hearth or the wood-burning stove where cooking is done for a whole family symbolizes the family unity. An iron pot of large dimensions is suspended on a heavy chain over the stove. All cooking is done in the same kitchen, even if the extended family includes 50 or more individuals.

Both the hearth and the chain above it are considered sacred to the Abkhasians. In the past, a man took an oath by placing his right hand on the family chain. When the pot in which the abista is cooked three times a day becomes too small to feed the whole family, the oldest son and his wife and children may separate and build themselves a new home next to that of the father. The people say that such a family has "broken its chain."

At the time of separation, a family feast takes place, and a sacrifice is made for good fortune. Members of the abipara are invited to the feast, as the separation is also their concern.

Yet one is never completely separate in Abkhasia. Just as no orphans are left destitute, there are no wandering beggars. No word for *beggar* exists in their language. When a man is impoverished due to misfortunes, his relatives and neighbors help him, and it is considered a shame to refuse help. If the people of his own village did not help him, then the next village would, and they would look down on those who were lacking in the important virtue of *apatys*, or conscience.

KINSHIP TERMINOLOGY

Abkhasian kinship terminology, which confuses an outsider at first glance, is actually based on a small number of roots. These are combined to indicate any position in the lineage of one's father, mother, or spouse. The basic terms are:

ab—father
an—mother
ascha—blood, from which is derived aescha, or brother
akhushcha—sister
apa—son, from which *ipa*, his son and *lpa*, her son
apkha—daughter, from which *ipkha*, his daughter and *lpkha*, her daughter
apkhus—wife
ankhua—not real, in-law
psa—instead of, step
anpsa—not real mother, stepmother

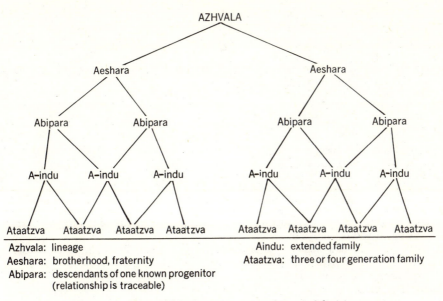

AZHVALA

Aeshara | Aeshara

Abipara | Abipara | Abipara | Abipara

A–indu | A–indu | A–indu | A–indu | A–indu | A–indu

Ataatzva | Ataatzva | Ataatzva | Ataatzva | Ataatzva | Ataatzva | Ataatzva | Ataatzva

Azhvala: lineage
Aeshara: brotherhood, fraternity
Abipara: descendants of one known progenitor
(relationship is traceable)

Aindu: extended family
Ataatzva: three or four generation family

Figure 1 *The Abkhasian Lineage and Its Subdivisions*

In addition, the prefix *s* indicates first person possessive, *a* indicates a noun, and the suffix *adu* means big (the English equivalent is *grand*). Thus, an Abkhasian will address members of his father's lineage as follows:

daddu—father of my father's grandfather; affectionate term for all old men from grandfather on
sabdu iab du iab—great-grandfather of my grandfather
sabdu iab iabdu—grandfather of my grandfather
sabdu iabdu—father of my grandfather
andu—grandmother (paternal or maternal)
aeshchadu—brother of my father's grandfather, literally big brother
abiascha—father's brother
sabieshaipa—my father's brother's son
sabieshaipkha—my father's brother's daughter
sash'a-ipa—my brother's son
sash'a-ipkha—my brother's daughter
spa-ipa—son of my son

Note that the terms for father's brother's children are the same as the terms for my brother's children, and both literally mean "son of my blood" and "daughter of my blood," indicating membership in the lineage over and above membership in a particular generation.

However, the children of women who are members of my lineage are themselves members of the lineages of their father's, not of my lineage:

abiakhush'a—father's sister (my lineage)
sabiakhusha-lpa—my father's sister's son (his father's lineage)
sabiakhuschalpkha—my father's sister's daughter (her father's lineage)
sakhsh'alpkha—daughter of my sister (her father's lineage)
apkha-lpa—daughter's son

Again, the terms for father's sister's daughter and my sister's daughter are the same, equating women who were born to members of my lineage.

Members of one's mother's lineage are addressed as follows:

aenshcha—mother's brother, his son, and all men who carry mother's family name, except her father
aenlakhsh'a—mother's sister, and all women who carry her name

Since the name is passed down through the father, *aenlakhsh'a* does not refer to the mother's sister's daughter, but does include any female children of men who carry the mother's name, although by English reckoning they may be considerably more distant. Also, the mother's brother's son is in her lineage, and is a closer relative than the mother's sister's son, who carries the name of his father.

Terms also exist to denote the spouses and children of other important relatives:

amakhu—husband of my daughter and all husbands of women who carry my family name; that is, a woman of my lineage
sakhsh'a-pkha—daughter of a woman who carries my family name; same as father's sister's daughter; that is, any woman who is *sakhsh'a-pkha* to me will carry the name of a man who is *amakhu* to me
sash's ipa ipkheys—wife of my brother's son
san lash'a ipa ipkheya—wife of my mother's brother's son, other relatives by marriage
abkhua—father-in-law (father not real)
ankhua—mother-in-law
sabkhua uan—my not real father's mother; that is, the paternal grandmother of my spouse
abkhunda—all men who carry my spouse's family name, except his or her father
ankhpkha—all women who carry spouse's family name, except his or her mother
sanpsa—my stepmother
spkhapsa—my stepdaughter

There are terms for stepfather and stepson, but these are rarely used, since children go with their father's lineage in case of death or divorce and are more likely to require a stepmother than a stepfather.

RITUAL KINSHIP

There are three kinds of permanent ritual kinship institutions in Abkhasia. These are:

atalyk—bringing up a child of another family with the intention of establishing kin relations between the members of both families.
milk brotherhood—ritually established between adults in order to cement friendships.
adoption—occurring when a family has no sons to perpetuate the family line, or because they want more children; adults are adopted to establish kin relations with a powerful group.

Since animosity in any form was not allowed within the family or clan, any aggressive feelings which might arise were allowed an outlet against members of another azhvala to which one was not related, or against people of other nationalities.

The term *atalyk* is used in ethnographic literature to describe a custom once practiced in the Caucasus. A boy or girl, shortly after birth, was usually given by a family of greater and social standing to one of a lesser position. However, families of equal standing could do so, as well.

Atalyk is a word of Turkic origin, and literally means one who brings up or educates a child not his own. In Soviet ethnographic literature, the custom is referred to as *atalychestvo*. The Abkhasian word for a man who raises another's child is *azara*, and the child is called *akhupkha*. The relationship is called *akhashvara* or, in different parts of Abkhasia, *akhashatera*.

This relationship was formally established by the appropriate ritual and exchange of gifts. In Abkhasia, this practice was widespread during the first decades of the twentieth century, declining only after the establishment of Soviet rule, and the abolition of the blood feud, which, among other things, eliminated the need for protection afforded by ritual relationships.

The akhupkha and his milk siblings (that is, children who were nursed by the same woman, or his adoptive siblings) were taught the same customs, skills, and manners, so that an Abkhasian peasant knew as much as a prince. To be brought up properly meant, for a boy, to become a heroic warrior, physically strong and courageous, able to use weapons and ride skillfully. He also had to be well-mannered, a fluent orator, and knowledgeable in Abkhasian lore. The girl was taught housework, spinning, weaving, and embroidery. For her, proper behavior meant modesty, respect, and self-control. Frequent slave raids by the Turks and other groups made it necessary for her to learn to ride and shoot as well.

The azara and his family were fully responsible for the safety and well-being of their charges. In return, they received gifts of money and horses from the natural parents. This obligation was taken so seriously that, when the house of the Shoniya family caught fire, the mother ran in and rescued their akhupkha, a child of the Lakrba family. She then tried to rescue her own baby, but it was too late, and the child perished in the flames. This act was considered quite praiseworthy, whereas if she had rescued her own child first, she would have been condemned.[2]

The link established between two families, one of which received the child of another, was considered sacred and even stronger than the bond of blood. Intermarriage between the two families, their relatives, and any people of the same surname was immediately forbidden. It was enough to mention to two people contemplating marriage that there was an atalyk relationship between their families in order to make the marriage impossible.

The children of the azara were considered milk brothers or milk sisters to the akhupkha. The new child became a member of his atalyk family. He ate, played, slept and worked with the other children of his atalyk parents. The duties of the milk brothers and sisters to the new child were spelled out; for instance, in times of war, the milk brother was to protect his akhupkha with his own body, to stand between him and the enemy, and to die first, if necessary. Much was forgiven the

[2] Sh. D. Inal-Ipa, *Abkhasia*. Sukhumi: Alashara, 1965, p. 483.

Milk siblings (two people nursed by the same woman), both 102 years old. Such bonds are as important as blood relationships in Abkhasia.

akhupkha, to the point where an obnoxious visitor could be told, "You allow yourself a lot of liberties, as if you were our akhupkha."

When the akhupkha came of age, his return home to his natural parents was celebrated by a great feast for all the relatives. His duty to his azara and his milk siblings continued for life. He protected them from any danger, and came to their assistance in time of need. In fact, all blood and ritual relationships involve lifetime obligations, and ritual kinship is not established lightly. By contrast, merely a sexual relationship, can be dissolved.

The atalyk served to cement ties between different families, to reduce the distance between social classes, to ensure uniformity of culture, and to make peace between feuding families. In the past, when a family was engaged in a feud and feared retaliation, they would sometimes kidnap a child and declare that they were going to raise it, thus automatically ending the hostilities. The parents of the child could not reclaim it and continue the feud, since the child in all probability had already been nursed, and milk is considered a sacred substance.

For example, two men, Bazal and Zantariya, had a quarrel about a piece of land. Zantariya beat up Bazal, and in retaliation, the son of Bazal wounded two members of Zantariya's family. In order to stop the feud, Bazal took an infant boy from Zantariya's family. One day, the brothers of Zantariya and boys from an allied family had a quarrel, and one of the Zantariya brothers was encouraged to continue the feud. Chincha, a boy from the allied family, killed Bazal.

People gathered to discuss the matter and, in the meantime, Chincha ran home and sat there playing an instrument. His parents signed a judgment against him, saying that they did not want to have a son who mixed milk with blood. The killer was exiled, never to return. The kidnaped boy remained in peace in Bazal's household and was raised by his adopted family.

Sometimes a child was even given to a non-Abkhasian tribe, in order to establish ties between the two groups. After the Revolution, the Soviets encouraged the institution of atalyk for a while, in order to create political harmony. They even established a special committee which concerned itself with feuds.

The atalyk is an institution of the past, but there are people in Duripsh who were brought up in this manner. Children are no longer given to other families to raise. An exception occurs where many children in a family have died and only one survives, or a new baby is born. The family arranges for some other family to kidnap the child and raise it, in order to avoid the evil spirits responsible for the previous deaths.

According to Soviet ethnographic theory as developed by M. O. Kosven, atalyk is one of the survivals of a form of avunculate.[3] In the far past, the child was given to the mother's relatives, especially the mother's brother. After the transition from matriarchy to patriarchy, with the strengthening of the patriarchal family, the child left only temporarily and then returned to the father's family. This, in the Caucasus, developed into atalyk. There the children were not given to relatives but to people who were economically or militarily dependent on the parents of the akhupkha. Therefore, they could be returned to their families.

Atalyk is not adoption, and although there are common elements in attitude and practice, the two institutions remain distinct in the Caucasus.

Even at present, there are many families in Duripsh who keep their kin ties with their milk brothers. Since ritual brotherhood was considered of the same strength and importance as blood relationships and was inherited for at least a couple of generations, and given the long lives and late marriages common in Abkhasia, these ties may persist for another century or two. Milk brothers and sisters will continue to visit each other, give presents, and help each other in need.

Adoption   Adoption is called *avnadara*, which literally means "receiving into the house" as one's own blood. The establishment of kin status between warring parties was, as we have mentioned, the most effective way to stop blood feuds, to win an ally, or to receive protection from an important personage.

The main feature of adoption of a stranger is a ritual in which he is allowed to put his lips to the breast of either the mother or the wife of the head of the family, making the stranger symbolically the son or daughter of the house.

Adopting a child and giving him the name of the adopted parents is widely practiced, even at the present time. The phrase is, "We made him our son." Often the Abkhasians, who love children, will adopt a child of a relative or even a

[3] M. O. Kosven, "The *Atalyk* Relationship," *Soviet Ethnography*, 1935, Vol. 2.

stranger, if they have none of their own. In former times, the child had to be taken from an Abkhasian, never a foreigner, and social class distinctions had to be observed. Later, these limitations disappeared. Very often, in a family of one or two children, a third will be adopted. During World War II, the Abkhasians took a number of children from Leningrad, which was under siege.

I once delivered a lecture at the Institute of Abkhasian Literature and Culture in Sukhumi. There were over a hundred students present. My topic was the importance of kinship systems in the understanding of cultures. I used theirs as an example.

At the end of the discussion I asked whether some of them could tell me offhand how many relatives they had. Immediately, there was a big show of hands as many students volunteered. The first student said that according to his grandfather, who is a member of the family council, they numbered 500. Another student said that her family was not such a large one, and only numbered around 350. Other people also responded with, seemingly to my ears, large numbers. They, in turn, asked me how many relatives I had in the United States. When I mentioned just a few, they looked at me with great sympathy. As an expression of their concern, they asked me whether I would like to be adopted into some large lineage, as is the custom for people as forlorn as I looked to them.

Milk Brotherhood   Sometimes two grown men decide to become milk brothers out of friendship. A man and a woman may form a similar relationship, if they are in love with each other but unable to marry. This permits them to kiss each other, go places together and be openly affectionate, though of course, they are still barred from sexual relationships.

The two men go through the ritual of joining little fingers together, and if neither has a wife or mother present, they put their lips to each other's breasts. After the ceremony, there is a banquet at which animals slaughtered for this purpose are served. The two brothers are given each a shouldercut, which is the most honorable portion of the animal, and they then exchange portions. Before they eat, an older man cuts a piece of meat from the shoulder and puts it into the mouth of the older brother, and then the younger. Afterwards, the rest of the shoulder is cut into pieces and all the people partake of it. There is an Abkhasian saying, ". . . the one who brought you into his house and fed you the shoulder of an animal slaughtered in your honor is your father, and his wife is your mother."

Considering all the rights and privileges extended to members of a family group, it was natural that homeless people and small, weak groups wanted to join the larger, more powerful families for protection and privileges. Deep insults, such as killing, bodily injury, or making advances towards the wrong women, resulted in conflicts which not only involved the injured individuals, but also their families, abiparas and azhvalas. Armed conflicts were not infrequent, since most males in former times carried one or two pistols and a dagger, with their hands ready at the hilt of the dagger as often as not. Since kinship is determined by birth, the numerous mechanisms for establishing fictitious kinship were invented in order to obtain allies or to provide for the cessation of hostilities.

Ritual kinship may be established by a family or by a whole community, and

Abkhasians are known to perform the ritual with wild animals which have been annoying their homes and livestock in order to gain the goodwill of the animal. I was told that in the community of Khlou, in the region of Khodor, a wolf often attacked the cows and lambs of a shepherd in the village. In desperation, the shepherd went to search for his enemy. It turned out to be a she-wolf with a litter of cubs. He killed the she-wolf but took the little ones to his house, and when they grew up he let them go free, hoping that as their azara, he would be immune to wolves and that they could not possibly harm him.

It is said that the shepherd even performed the ritual, his wife sitting on a chair and permitting the cubs to touch her breasts, giving them the status of sons. Since then, the story goes, the wolves never touched his cattle and the shepherd never killed wolves. Mindful of his forest family, he always left some food in the forest for them.

The theme of milk relatives appears frequently in Abkhasian folklore. People felt that it was quite possible to make anyone a milk relative, from a wolf to a god.

In the spring of 1914, an epidemic of smallpox spread through the Abkhasian villages. Supplies of vaccine were distributed all over the countryside. But the villagers of Dzhgerda, fearing that the god of smallpox would be offended and punish them, refused to undergo the vaccination. They decided instead to adopt the god, knowing that he could not harm his relatives.

Each family contributed money for the purchase of two sacrificial goats, which were snow-white and without blemish. Bearing food with them, the entire village, young and old of both sexes, went into the woods to perform the ceremony. The eldest male sacrificed the animals after an appropriate prayer.

The people also brought two beds covered with silk blankets, upon which two women were seated. One was a representative of the peasantry, the other of the nobility, and they had been selected as the most beautiful and virtuous of each class. Their dresses were opened to expose their breasts to the god, but for modesty's sake, they were covered with silk kerchiefs. Everyone kneeled and the eldest man made a speech inviting the god to accept the sacrifice of the goats, and imploring him to put his lips to the breasts of the women to signify that he accepted them as milk relatives. After this ritual, a feast followed. And it is said that the villagers of Dzhgerda were protected from smallpox from that day on.[4]

RITUAL KINSHIP AS A BARRIER TO MARRIAGE

The prohibition of marriage between wet-nurse and baby, and the nurse's children, exists also in Moslem law. It is extended to the other children who were nursed by the women, and in Abkhasia, between the child and his descending line on the one side and the nursing woman's on the other, with all blood and milk relatives of this woman and her husband. This prohibition is considerably softened at the present time, and the young people claim that while it is prohibited to

[4] Sh. D. Inal-Ipa, "The Social Function of *Atalyk* Relationships in Nineteenth-Century Abkhasia," in *Works of the Abkhasian Institute of Language, Literature, and History*, vol. XXV. Sukhumi: Alashara, 1955.

marry milk brothers and sisters, they can marry the brothers and sisters of milk brothers and especially their cousins.

Adoption and ritual brotherhood between adults are also a barrier to marriage. Unlike Moslem law, where wet-nursing (actual or symbolic) is not a crucial factor in adoption, it is essential to legitimize an Abkhasian adoption. None of the members of the family into which the baby is adopted can marry any member of the original family of the adopted child. The links connecting ritual brothers are also considered sacred. Among all the people of the Caucasus, with the exception of the Christian Ossetians, the members of the families of these brothers can not intermarry.

Some limitations on marriage were connected with less important relationships. If somebody cuts the hair of a child on the day he is one year old, he is considered a godfather to the baby, and his own children cannot marry the child who had the haircut. However, this relationship is not as important as one legitimized by that sacred fluid, milk.

SENIOR RELATIVES BY MARRIAGE

A woman may not speak to her father-in-law, nor may he hear the sound of her voice. He may decide after a number of years that he wishes to speak to her. He then gives a feast where he offers her presents, and asks her to speak to him. This feast, in the presence of witnesses, shows everyone that she is permitted to speak to him. A story is told of a man who had given such a feast, but finding that his daughter-in-law was unbearably talkative, he had to give another feast, with many more presents, in order to persuade her to resume her silence.

Since the relationship between a man and his daughter-in-law is distant in Abkhasian society, it is quite possible that the restrictions on their communication are unusually strong in order to avoid any temptation to commit incest. While the son continues to live in his father's house for some years after marriage, his father cannot exercise arbitrary authority over him, and the son is free to leave whenever he likes. In this way, the family is kept together as a unit, while envy and competition between father and son are reduced or eliminated.

A woman does not speak to her mother-in-law for a brief period after marriage, but this interval is quite short, because a young bride is a newly acquired servant in the house and must be given directions. The daughters-in-law in a household are ranked in accordance with the relative ages of their husbands, and the respect each daughter-in-law owes to the next no doubt parallels that shown between the younger and older brother, and between a man and his father.

Marriage is not as sacred or permanent as blood or milk relationships. When a woman leaves her lineage in order to marry, her father must ask the spirits to grant her permission. She still remains a member of her own lineage, and her family is careful to defend her rights against abuse from her husband or his family. Should she be mistreated, her brother is the first to defend her, initiating a blood feud between the two families. This is the most likely explanation for a man's deference to his wife's senior relatives, in particular to her brother.

The woman's son is a blood relation to her lineage, and the closest relative to her brother. This tie cannot be broken, and there is no possibility of bloodshed between the two.

AVOIDING TROUBLE BETWEEN GENERATIONS

As an Abkhasian grows older, more and more family privileges are extended to him, regardless of his wealth or occupation. This could give rise to hostility between the younger and older generations, but the following mechanisms serve to alleviate resentment:

1. Each Abkhasian knows that he will eventually receive the same privileges in his turn, in accordance with age and sex. There is no need to compete for privileges; in fact, one cannot obtain them by competition.

2. The elders are avoided, so as to reduce the occasions which give rise to resentment. Restricting the interaction between generations to that which is prescribed by the rules transforms a potentially explosive situation into a life style which the younger people find not only tolerable, but even desirable.

3. Behavior and expectations are formalized. The older person receives certain privileges, but these are limited by the rules, and the younger generation is not subject to the whims of aging despots. The code of behavior is applied objectively, without favoritism, and children are never confused as to what is expected of them or how much they can get away with.

4. The peer group is cooperative, and does not compete for the favors of the older generation. The peer group provides a refuge from tension, and provides a situation in which one can be comfortable.

5. The older generation does not intrude on the youth. Young people are free to choose their own careers, to succeed or to fail without altering their relationships to their elders in any way. By not interfering, the parents avoid not only resentment directed against them, but also sibling rivalry.

PARENTS AND CHILDREN

Children may not talk to their parents in the presence of the grandparent or senior relatives. The father especially should not be seen playing with his child and talking to him, and it is also not proper to mourn publicly for one's own dead child. However, relatives other than the parents may play with the child in public, and may openly display grief if he dies. This custom persists down to the present day. Inal-Ipa (1954) writes of an old man who, in the presence of his older brother's widow, did not permit his own sons to come close to him, nor allow them to pour water when he washed his hands.[5]

These rules encourage the individual to relate to the extended family as a

---

[5] Sh. D. Inal-Ipa, *Studies in the History of Marriage and the Family in Abkhasia.* Sukhumi: Abgiz, 1954, p. 60.

whole, rather than forming excessively dependent attachments to his parents. From earliest infancy, the Abkhasian child is shown affection by his parents in private, but in public situations, he learns that he will only get attention from other relatives, and their manifestations of affection for him produce intense feeling and loyalty.

HUSBAND AND WIFE

A husband and wife may not call each other by name in the presence of senior relatives, sit next to one another, or talk to one another at all in the presence of strangers. A young bride sends messages to her husband through children or youngsters, or speaks generally if she wishes to convey some information, saying, "One should . . . ." She is not supposed to speak to him directly, in the presence of others, and it is improper for them to show feelings of love or concern for each other, or even to mourn the death of one's spouse.

A wife may not even use her husband's name. My Abkhasian assistant, in order to demonstrate the force of this custom, asked a young woman for the name of her husband. She replied, "You know I am not permitted to mention it." This, in spite of the fact that she was an outstanding political leader.

One can hypothesize that the intense passions which may arise out of a sexual relationship must always be subordinated to the necessity of the lineage to function as a unit, without internal conflict. The young bride is always a stranger in the house, and is a threat insofar as there exists the possibility that her husband's passion for her will weaken his loyalty to his lineage. Abkhasian fiction is replete with tales of conflicts between one's loyalty to one's family and the desire for a marriage not approved of by the elders, so we can assume that this is an area where feelings are not easily overcome.

FEUDS

There was considerable movement among the population within Abkhasia before the Revolution. One of the most pressing reasons for moving (either as an individual or with one's entire family) was to escape blood revenge. When a murder was committed, the murderer and his entire lineage were in mortal danger if they remained in the vicinity. Often they escaped to Georgia or the northern Caucasus. Once, I was told, a man fled to the United States; but after a few years, a relative of the murdered man caught up with him and took his life.

Many peasants who escaped from feuds in one community became dependent on landlords in another because, according to the rules of hospitality, the landlord must protect a man who comes to his land.

Blood feuds were begun by murder, physical assault, stealing of cattle, stealing or insulting women, or broken promises. One of the most frequent causes of feuds was an insult to a woman, or sleeping with a young woman and then refusing to marry her. Thus, when questioned about the cause of a feud, an Abkhasian may say, "Oh, it was a woman's tail." He will then explain this to a foreigner by saying that a woman was involved, and the "tail" is a reference to the fact that a feud may continue between families for a long time, following after the woman like a tail. It is likely that the phrase has sexual connotations as well.

Although the custom is not quite dead yet, and may occasionally flare up, it is nevertheless difficult to imagine the tragedy and terrible fanaticism which once accompanied blood feuds. According to the adats, the blood revenge had to take place within three days after the murder of a man, and before the body is buried. Obviously, this was not always possible. The closest male relative was and is the avenger—father, brothers, maternal uncles, cousins, and milk brothers. Not to take vengeance is the greatest disgrace conceivable, and a man who does not perform his duty is a subject of contempt. Vengeance is always taken upon the males of a particular lineage, never on females, and females do not take part in vengeance. If no close relative is available, a distant one will do. Old men are not usually chosen for this task, though.

In the past, the relative chosen by the family to be the avenger was completely isolated from the life around him until he fulfilled his duty. He covered his face with his bashlick and left the house. He could not return, or take part in festivities, marry, work to care for his family, or participate in the funeral of a deceased. Before leaving the house, he made a short speech.

> My people, I should die instead of you. Today we send my brother on his last journey. _____ took his life, and now the bullet and the blood is between us and calls for revenge. I will not cry for my brother on the day that we part forever; but I swear before God and before you that shortly I will place on his grave the right hand of the man who, in his evil desire, took my brother's life.

Even under these dire circumstances, certain rules had to be followed. If the murderer met the avenger, he could not attack first, but could only defend himself. If he met the avenger in a public place, he had to leave immediately. The avenger also had the right to the first shot. To shoot or stab an enemy in the back is still not considered manly. The type of weapon used was also important; for example, to kill a man with a stick instead of a dagger or a gun was adding insult to injury.

A story is told of a murderer who had been in hiding for a long time, and who came home to bathe and change his clothes. As he undressed, his wife expressed the fear that the avenger might take advantage of his weaponless condition and shoot him. To this, he answered, "No, my enemy is not the kind of person who would shoot a naked man." And sure enough, his enemy had followed him to the house, but on seeing a naked man through the window, he turned around and left.

Once a man had avenged his relative, he had to treat the body of his enemy with respect, covering it with a cape and tying the dead man's horse to a tree. The horse had to be available to participate in its master's funeral. Then he had to go to the grave of the relative whom he had avenged and announce that he had performed his duty.

In the nineteenth century, money payment was substituted for blood. The price depended on the social class of the victim. The feud was concluded only when the two lineages became relatives: the injured family had to adopt the murderer, or the murderer's relatives had to adopt a baby from the new family. Sometimes, when the family of the victim refused to make peace with the family of the murderer, the murderer's family might conspire in some way to take the child, and this would end the feud. These feuds are not merely ancient history; in 1924, the families of Amichba and Ashiba were joined in marriage, thus ending the feud between them. By that time, eleven men had been killed.

It was and is possible for feuding families to change their feelings about each other immediately upon such a settlement, for the lineages share common feelings and a common life style. There was no basic disagreement about beliefs.

While a man was always required to exact vengeance, he did not necessarily have to take the life of his enemy. The Abkhasians have ways of avenging insults and releasing aggression which are less serious than murder; and ways of ending hostilities when each side considers itself "even." Inal-Ipa interviewed a hundred-year-old man, Tamshug Kapba, who says that he himself witnessed these events: once a year, the peasants, the lesser nobility, and even some higher-ranking nobles were supposed to visit the homestead of Prince Uchardiya Dzyapsh-ipa and shake his hand as an indication of their fealty. For some reason, a peasant named Marshan Daltykva refused to do it one year. The prince avenged himself for this snub by shooting a cow which belonged to Daltykva's milk brother—a worse insult than shooting the man's own cow. Daltykva then shot the prince's cow, and the reckoning was considered complete at that point.[6]

[6] Sh. D. Inal-Ipa, 1955, p. 103.

5/The Abkhasian family

CHILDREN

The love of children does not induce Abkhasians to have large families. An Abkhasian couple rarely has more than two children. A 1963 survey of the village of Atara-Abkhaskaya revealed that 60 percent of all peasant households had either one or two children, while 8.1 percent had no children at all. Two percent of the households had adopted one or two children, and only 12 percent had more than five children.[1] Late marriage and a conserving of energy may account for this.

The small family may be an adaptation to past conditions of frequent warfare. It was important to be able to travel quickly and lightly. Large numbers of youngsters would have been a handicap to a family fleeing to the mountains to avoid being captured by slave raiders. In addition, the pastoral economy of pre-Revolutionary days required fewer workers than does an agricultural one. Moreover, the Abkhasian land could not support large families. At present, the population seems to be increasing, and young people tend to have more children than their parents did.

Children are desired, especially boys, since they provide continuity in the patrilineal system. But the act of having children does not validate masculinity or femininity. For a woman, her child is a focus of interest, someone she commands and who obeys unconditionally, and to whom she can give unrestricted affection in the privacy of her own room. However, her authority is restricted by the rules, as with all elders in Abkhasian society, and she can never give arbitrary orders.

Many Abkhasians with whom I spoke mentioned their mothers with deep feeling. A man of my acquaintance, much pressed for time, was requested by his mother to meet her in a neighboring village. I asked him if he would go. "I must," he replied. "To me she is holy."

An Abkhasian baby does not "belong" to its parents but more to the family as a whole. All of the family, the aunts, grandmother, and elder sisters, impart affection but not constant minute attention on the infant. The mother rarely touches her

[1] Ts. N. Bzhaniya, "Family and Family Life in an Abkhasian Collective Village," in L. Kh. Akaba and Sh. D. Inal-Ipa (eds.), *The Contemporary Abkhasian Village*. Tbilisi: Metzniereba Publishers, 1967, p. 7.

baby, cuddling it only when there is no one around. She does not even pick it up in breast feeding; instead, she bends over the cradle to nurse.

When I asked to see one of the infants bound in its cradle, my friend took me to the home of a "sister" of his (that is, a female member of his lineage) and her newborn baby. A woman picked up the infant and proudly displayed him around the crowded room.

"You have a beautiful child," I remarked to the woman.

"Oh, that isn't her child," my friend said. "She's an aunt. The mother is over there in the corner."

The baby spends the first six months of his life in a cradle. This ingenious contraption is made of wood, with a hay or straw mattress and a hole in the bottom. Two strips of cloth are attached to each side of the crib, then fastened around the baby's chest and hips, rendering him quite immobile. A bamboo tube leads from the private parts down through the hole, emptying into a bucket below. The baby is taken out a few times a day—but never for nursing nor in response to his crying. After six months, however, he is only bound when he is sleeping.

Children are nursed for two or three years, though in the past, they might nurse up to five years. Supplementary feeding of cornmeal mush, buttermilk, and fresh milk begins at eight months, and by the end of the first year, the child is eating the same food as the rest of the family, including the local wine. Food is served at regular intervals, taken in moderation, and chewed thoroughly. Children are not encouraged to overeat, which is considered unhealthy.

The parents are quite concerned about the health of their child. Ritual and medical precautions assure proper development. But the child, as much as the parents, becomes responsible for his own health. Children are made to appreciate and to understand the importance of maintaining health and preventing disease.

Sickness is not considered a normal occurrence. However, if one has sinned, sickness may be linked to the misdeed. In greeting one asks, "How is your health?" and the answer may well be, "I am healthy. I am not guilty of anything." There is no regression to childhood attitudes as in Western societies where children and very old people do not expect to live up fully to the normal code of behavior when they are not well. Among the Abkhasians, neither children nor old people use sickness as an excuse from duty or to relax rules.

A baby is cared for, but growing children are given considerable personal autonomy and are expected to take care of themselves. A child is not questioned about elimination. He must not dirty the floor, his clothes, or the courtyard. Since toilets are located at some distance from the house, he must learn to go there in time. Rapid changes in temperature are taken for granted in the mountains, and the children decide for themselves when they need extra clothing, without adults worrying about them catching colds.

Until age seven or eight, children are not expected to observe strict standards of cleanliness or self-restraint. The code is then applied objectively, without considerations of favoritism or individual temperament. This results in a strong sense of security.

The stoicism that Abkhasian culture demands is instilled conscientiously in almost every aspect of growing up and growing old by the parents and senior relatives. While the rules are somewhat relaxed at present, it is still considered improper or in bad taste to show one's feelings for husband or wife, or for one's children in the presence of relatives. However, one can show feelings in relation to other people in public.

"It is for the good of the children that the parents are willing to deprive themselves of the pleasure of kissing and hugging," remarked one grandmother.

The father does not hold, fondle, or kiss the child very much, and never in the presence of others. I was told the story of a man who attended a meeting outdoors, while his three-year-old son played nearby. The boy, without thinking, moved nearer and nearer to the edge of an overhang. Finally, the father stepped on the boy's shirt and pinned him in this manner, without ceasing to converse with the other adults present. An older sibling noticed the predicament and picked up the child. The father's behavior was considered quite praiseworthy.

Nonetheless, the father is not absent. The family eats together and works together very often, not out of "togetherness" but out of necessity.

A child's physical and emotional security derive from the conviction that his needs are going to be met by any of the members of his large household, and even by his neighbors. He is involved with a great many people. As he gets older and begins to visit neighboring homes, he is accepted and treated as their own child.

Yet the Abkhasian child is subject to stern parental demands that shape the stoic attitude characteristic of the people. To an outsider, the rules of behavior seem rigid and difficult; however, they are imposed consistently from the beginning. Children are never confused as to what is expected of them or how much they will be able to "get away with." Good behavior is rewarded by praise, but never by suspension of rules.

Children obey instantly. I never heard a child cry in protest or a parent raise his voice or threaten spanking. A command is never repeated twice. As a teacher of fidgety American youth, I marveled at Abkhasian schoolchildren who are required to sit at rigid attention for hours. Some anthropologists attribute this composure to the experience of being confined in the cradle in babyhood. Such miraculous results are not motivated by fear. Respect is the key, and this adult concept is conveyed to little children and reinforced by showing over and over again the correct adult example. Thus the young learn they must obey the same rules as the old.

A parent expresses disapproval by withholding praise, which is otherwise very generously dispensed. The Abkhasian concept of discipline, considered necessary and good for children, is not intertwined with the concept of punishment. Abkhasians feel that physical punishment induces disrespect. This may be the reason for so little resentment between the generations: the Abkhasian method of discipline does not allow for the development and expression of even the mildest forms of sadistic impulse. Also, with no threat of punishment there is less attempt on the part of the child to see how far he can go.

For example, a young man whom I knew to be a very warm and loving father repeatedly pushed his three-year-old son away from him when his own mother was present. He did not yell or give in when the child persisted. Each time the child approached him, he would remind him that his grandmother was present. Finally, the boy gave up because he knew that no effort on his part could achieve the results that he wanted. The children learn early in life not to beat their heads against brick walls.

On another occasion, a friend of mine kissed his children good-bye. His wife and I were present. The youngest, a three-year-old, asked him why he didn't kiss their mother, too.

"Don't you love Mommy?" the boy asked.

"Yes, I love Mommy," his father replied, "but I don't kiss her when other people are watching. I can only kiss her when no one else is present. But I love Mommy very much."

Abkhasian rules provide for courteous behavior, for showing respect and receiving it. Ill temper courts disaster. Moods, physical indispositions, and so on are not excuses for outbursts or harsh words. Abkhasians feel positive revulsion against boorish behavior. They do not place emotional obstacles before themselves; at the most difficult tasks, my Abkhasian assistants would first say, "Well, let's try."

Training in modesty comes early. Privacy, even in the family community, is prized, and at adolescence, youths are given their own rooms or, if the main house is filled, a small hut in the yard.

When very small children bathe, the boys are separated from the girls, and the feeling of shame in connection with physical exposure is very strong. There is no training in guilt, however, although girls are more restricted in speech and behavior, the restrictions are introduced after the age of seven or eight, when a sense of security has already been established. Though extreme modesty is expected, it is made possible by the special care taken to provide each individual with some measure of privacy in dressing, sleeping, washing, and so on, no matter how many individuals live in the household.

Work is considered good and necessary, and children are trained from an early age to participate in household tasks. Later on, they work with their families collecting tea leaves, beginning at the preschool level and continuing on all days when they are free from school. The Abkhasians have not become so ambitious as to overwork themselves and their children, however.

The division of labor starts early. A five-year-old boy refused to bring me a broom on request, because this was "woman's work." He would not even touch it.

Slaughtering animals is taught to small boys. An animal slaughtered by a woman is considered unfit for human consumption. Therefore, when there is no man in the house, a little boy may have to kill a chicken. Once, I visited an Abkhasian household where a woman had to prepare dinner when no adult males were present. The woman put a knife in the hand of her four-year-old son, held him, and drew the knife across the throat of the chicken, thus keeping to the letter of the law.

Both boys and girls are taught to carve meat properly. Abkhasians dislike any form of sloppy work, and if meat is carved in a way which is not in accordance with the prescribed pattern, it is considered almost indecent.

A girl of twelve is supposed to know all types of housework, and to look after the younger siblings. During mealtimes, and when guests are present, the young children always serve the older people. Small children eat separately, with their mothers. The adolescents stand behind the adults, pour wine, and attend to their needs.

Child-rearing techniques are geared to the development of strong, dependable adults who can master the weakness of both flesh and spirit, who fear neither life nor death, and who can hold their own in a harshly conceived world.

Once my friend Omar and I took his wife and daughter, Rima, on a trip to a lakeside resort about one hundred miles from their home. After about an hour's drive, I turned to talk to Rima in the back seat of the car and saw that she was pale from carsickness. At my suggestion, he stopped to let her rest.

"It's a pity," said Omar, "but if Rima becomes ill again, we will have to leave her at her grandmother's about twenty miles up the road."

I saw a look of determination come across Rima's face. Neither she nor her mother said a word, but I knew Rima would not allow herself to be ill, and she was not.

"Would you really have left your daughter behind?" I asked.

"If a man does not do what he says," he replied, "who would respect him?"

I asked Rima how she was able to control her carsickness. She replied that she simply did not want to miss the trip, and besides, it was humiliating to be sick. It was a sign of weakness.

To bear pain well is honorable, though the Abkhasians are not neglectful of injuries.

In Abkhasia, there is no change of standards with age. There is no point at which the children are given a body of information and ritual which has hitherto been kept secret from them. There are no separate "facts of life" for children and adults. The values given children are the ones adults live by, and there is no hypocritical disparity between adult words and deeds. Since what they are taught is considered important, and the work that they are given is necessary, children are neither rebellious nor restless.

In Abkhasia, older siblings quickly internalize their parents' standards by having to enforce them on the younger ones. The hierarchy of age extends down to the wobbliest toddler. A ten-year-old washes his hands first, then sees to it that his little brother washes his also before coming to the table. No one remains on the bottom of the heap for long, but each soon becomes a supervisor over others.

Ridicule is not used as a pedagogical tool in Abkhasia. Scorn and rejection are reserved for failure in family morals and not for failure to achieve. Neither sex is subject to physical punishment, nor to physical coercion. This no doubt bears some relation to the lack of intragroup violence in Abkhasia and the absence of rape.

The children are not excluded from any family functions or other aspects of life even though there is little conversation between the young and the old. A young Abkhasian who has to interrupt the speech of an elder will apologize by saying, "I cut your speech with gold." A disagreement is settled by a re-examination of the evidence. The elder's authority is simply not challenged, so questions of fact are not lost in an emotional struggle for power.

ADOLESCENCE

Ceremonies, such as *rites de passage*, which are designed to separate the various age groups, are not present in Abkhasian culture; and as far as can be ascertained, they never were. Life is viewed as a continuous curve of development. In contrast, the Western conceptualization is of a series of stages, from Shakespeare's Seven Ages of Man to the developmental stages of Freud and Erikson.

The days flow gradually from one to the next in Abkhasia, without the punctuation of harvest festivals, carnivals, or even birthdays. However, the influence of Russian culture and the structure imposed by the school system have introduced some new demarcations of time.

Even so, no initiation rite has developed to separate children from their mothers, boys from girls, and boys from men. None is necessary. The development of masculine or feminine virtues begins in the cradle. The mother nurses by bending over the crib and letting her child have the breast, rather than holding the child. A high degree of physical intimacy is not allowed to develop. Most of the time, the baby is carried by relatives other than the mother. As soon as a boy can move around, he follows his father, and a girl follows her mother; thus, sex role assignments are made clear from the beginning, and are never challenged.

In a culture which is more indulgent with its children, a young man must wrench himself away from his mother and prove his masculinity at a certain age. The Abkhasian male has gradually been led along the path to masculine achievement, and has been fitted to endure considerable physical stress without having to undergo the emotional shock of a sudden change in life style at puberty.

Puberty is not marked. At that time, the young people become intensely involved in sports, dancing and courting, but they never touch those of the opposite sex whom they are eligible to marry. The boys show off as sportsmen (there is competition on this level) and the girls sit around and admire them. Their courtships are quite prolonged and very romantic, with a great deal of fantasy. Little things are exaggerated—a glance, a chance encounter on the street—for it's a long, long way from courtship to the marriage bed.

Young women are not always passive spectators, however. They are expected to have a great deal of stamina and endurance. To be a really good dancer, a girl should be able to wear out three male partners since the steps he is required to perform are more strenuous. Physical fitness and beauty are important for both sexes.

In the upbringing of a young woman, great care is taken to make her as beautiful as possible according to Abkhasian standards. In order to narrow her waist and keep her breasts small, she wears a leather corset around her chest and waist which is permanently removed on her wedding night. Her complexion should be fair, her eyebrows thin, and her forehead high. This is accomplished by plucking the hair over her brow and preventing further growth through the application of certain bleaches and herbs.

When a girl reaches thirteen, she is expected to assume responsibility for looking after her own beauty. She uses mercurial ointment on her face. She boils *alicha*

(*Prunus divaricata*) and puts the foam on her face to whiten the skin. Cornstarch serves as face powder and as a skin softener. White clay is used as shampoo.

When I remarked on the beauty of Abkhasian women, I was told, "Oh yes, but the most beautiful were abducted and sold into slavery. Now we are trying to improve ourselves again and the women are growing more beautiful."

In general, young people remain quite close to their parents. This is especially true for young women. Male students or young workers may commute or live in rented rooms, but they return home at every opportunity. Since women *must* marry from their parent's home, they cannot live alone or even with other families in the cities as is possible in some western nations.

I kept asking young people why they accepted all the strict rules and requirements of their culture without rebellion. They said that if they did not do so they could no longer live in the village. They love the landscape of their villages. They enjoy the free air and feel that in the big cities like Sukhumi, which has three-story buildings, breathing is difficult because the buildings overshadow everything.

Another factor is the feeling of security that a very structured environment gives them. They can anticipate every move in the behavior of friends and enemies. Other nationalities, they say, are unpredictable. One has to rely on personal friendships and impressions. In Abkhasia, help and understanding are not left to personal choice, but decreed by the kinship system which embraces every individual. No one is disinherited, no one's place is insecure, not even a criminal. Only those who commit incest are socially outcast.

The Abkhasian never feels forgotten by his family. He cooperates rather than competes because his recognition and respect come through his family and his assigned place in it. He does not exist outside of it. Within the family, he is an individual, known for his unique characteristics. He participates not in terms of moral choices—there are indeed very few for an Abkhasian—but in terms of established and tested values which have persisted for centuries.

MARRIAGE

An Abkhasian Wedding   The Abkhasian wedding involves months of preparation, the heroic labors of the groom's family and all his neighbors, barrels full of wine, a herd of oxen, and multitudes of chickens. It is one of the high points of Abkhasian life, and is celebrated in legend and poetry. The following description is translated from a poem by Konstantin Lomia.

Abkhasian Wedding

Abkhasian wedding:
It's gay and noisy;
neither hall nor house
can contain it.

They dance!
The voices of our youth

fill the courtyard;
you can fill your eyes
watching the young people
work on the wedding.
And you can guess
what's on the table.

Adzhika storms your mouth
like liquid flame
the chickens are glazed,
khachapuri[2] is arranged
around a plate—
and here comes the abista!

Our own Tamada,
the host of the table,
asks, "Is it all ready?"
Yes, ready, everything, ready!

The first speech.
An honored clansman rises
like an ancient cliff.
Attention!

"Here's what I'll tell you
in this happy hour:

Let this young couple, throughout life,
be ignorant of sorrow.

"Let them not age with the years,
but shine forever like the sun
and moon.
Drink to them!
Let them be pure, transparent
as a mountain stream."

He finished
and drained his glass.

Abkhasian wedding!
If you want to know
true gaiety,
come to the wedding
which calls to you
with feasting, song, and dance.

The wedding always takes place in the groom's home, and always at his family's expense. Weeks before the actual celebration, the groom and his best man must go to the homestead of each prospective guest and personally issue invitations. The invitation proceeding is long and involves considerable traveling; the guest list is lengthy and the territory which the two men must cover to reach the widely scattered homesteads and villages is vast. Their departure from their home is celebrated ritually, with food, drink, and a prayer from the head of the household.

The bride must not show herself to outsiders before the big wedding. An intermediate stage used to provide for the bride's transition between leaving her own family and entering into her husband's new family. The bride was brought to her husband's relatives' home as a temporary stopover (*atatzadgala*) for a few days or weeks, until the wedding was ready. Such a step was necessary to prepare the bride, her new relatives, and the protective spirits of the house to receive the new member.

Now, the future bride is brought straight into her husband's family home. The groom's senior relatives and friends come to her father's household to escort her to the wedding. A small feast ensues with drinking and speech-making lasting a few hours. The groom's family also must pay for this small feast. The bride then rides on horseback or travels by car to the groom's household. Her parents and family must not attend the wedding. She is only accompanied by her bridesmaids and a male friend or relative of her own age who sees that her rights are protected. At some distance from her future home, the wedding party proceeds on foot into the courtyard to the house.

The wedding to which I was invited took place in the village of Aatzi, in 1970. My companions, one of whom was a relative of the groom, and I arrived in the early afternoon. As we drove to the village, we passed a considerable number of cars and flatbed trucks, full of people singing and waving to us. They were obviously returning from the wedding.

"Are we too late?" I asked.

[2] Khachapuri is a cheese-filled pastry, similar to Danish, but baked without sugar.

"Oh, no," my friend replied. "The wedding will go on until late at night."

As I later discovered, close to 1500 people attended, and it was necessary to entertain them in shifts.

We were met at the entrance of the courtyard by the groom's father and some other relatives, who invited us to have a look at the tent. In the open courtyard, a tent as long as a city block was erected, and long narrow tables placed inside it. The tent is very expensive and often is owned by the whole collective, to be lent to the members when needed. Men and women sat separately. As soon as one group of people finished eating, they were replaced by the next arrivals; and in spite of the large numbers involved, there was no confusion. Numerous appointed marshalls conscientiously attended to their specific tasks and made sure that everything ran smoothly.

The wedding gifts were carefully laid out on a bed on the porch so that the guests could see them. There were eighty-nine blankets and dozens of pillows. I wondered why there were so many of the same gifts, and was told that these would last a lifetime, for a couple, their children, and their guests. The best man dutifully registered each gift in a book, which the couple keeps for the rest of their lives. Every contributor made a short speech demeaning his gift before he named it. Then he drank to the health of the newlyweds, and the registrar rose while he was talking and drank with them. The gifts to the young couple can sometimes be cattle, furniture, or carpets. Small gifts are also given to the guests by the family of the groom.

During the wedding, the bride stood silently in a corner of a side room where the guests came to look at her and speak to her. It should be noted that there is no ceremony of joining the couple; the public feast is considered sufficient to signify to one and all that they are married. She wore an off-white nylon knit suit in the latest Soviet style, and a light veil was covering her face. However, she did not utter a sound or smile. The questions directed to her were answered by the bridesmaids who stood next to her and fended off jokes and remarks intended to provoke a smile or retort from the bride. It was a point of honor for her to maintain this silent composure.

She was supposed to stand there as long as the wedding continued, and her only relief came when her friends took her into another room to change her shoes to relieve her tired feet. Women have been known to faint at their weddings. The bride is not permitted to participate in the merry-making, and the groom must remain hidden in a friend's house, where he feasts with his peers.

Later, we sat down at a table inside the house, and various important guests came and introduced themselves to me. Suddenly a man entered the room on horseback, which surprised me so much that I dropped my "honorable portion" of chicken. He was greeted with exclamations of approval, for bringing a horse up the stairs is no easy feat. He had come to ask permission to "play," that is to give an exhibition of horsemanship. When the courtyard was not too crowded, permission would be granted. One of the women showed her appreciation of the horseman's feat by giving him a gift, an embroidered towel, which she tied to the front of his saddle. The rider then walked his horse gingerly down the steps of the porch and we followed to watch.

Afterwards, both men and women exhibited their skills at dancing. The guests formed a circle, clapping hands to the rhythm of the stringed music. A boy of about fourteen came out of the crowd and began to move slowly and then faster around the circle. He stamped his feet on the ground and raised himself on his toes. In a couple of minutes, a young girl about the boy's same age joined him in the dance. She glided within the circle moving her arms gracefully in the air. This was a courting dance. I was told that a traditional dance ends when the girl drops her handkerchief as a sign of submission and the boy pierces it with his dagger. When dancing, a girl and boy never touch each other. In former times, the rule was so strict that if her scarf floated out so that the boy dancing around her touched it, her family would take offense. After the courting dance had ended, many more people joined in the dances, including a very elderly gentleman who quite skillfully performed the steps.

The father of the groom came over to me after the dance and invited me to be introduced to the cooks. The male cooks are also considered important guests. They are neighbors of the groom, and they work incessantly, slaughtering and cooking the meat. Their wives cooked all but the meat and served the table. When I went out in the back, I saw huge spits turning, cauldrons bubbling, and the "honorable" hearts, livers and other parts hanging from the branches of a tree. Each of the cooks washed and then shook hands with me.

Just before the wedding, when everything is ready, all who participate in the preparations have a small feast of their own. A young bull is killed and the cooks sit down at the table with the members of the family to celebrate. Another celebration takes place after the tent is dismantled.

The food served consisted of the usual Abkhasian fare, including a few festive items, like factory-made cookies and khachapuri. I was expected to taste everything and to drink a full glass with each toast to the couple or to Abkhasia.

After a while, I asked the Chairman of the Collective, who sat next to me, to be excused because I am not used to drinking so much. He gave a command in Abkhasian, which saved me for a while; but his orders were soon forgotten, and my glass was filled again.

Weddings are great occasions for the young people to meet. In fact, parents are very eager to send their marriageable children to any social event so that they can meet friends and relatives, court, and learn more of the customs and laws of the Abkhasian people. Most young men are encouraged not to travel alone but as members of groups, performing duties such as taking part in the groom's retinue calling for the bride.

In the past, the father alone had the right to choose a mate for his child, particularly for his daughter. Refusal to marry was not only a rejection of the suitor, but also an insult to the father. A payment called *kalym* was made to the bride's family, to purchase her dowry. Formerly, the bride purchase was given in horses, sheep or cattle, but at present, money or other goods may be substituted. Marriages between people of different social strata were frowned upon. The children did not take the rights of the upper class parent, but of the lower.

Sometimes, marriages were arranged between young children, who were to be wed when they grew up. These promises were taken seriously, so that if the little girl died, the intended groom's family would wear mourning and pay for the funeral.

Stealing the bride is not a common occurrence in Abkhasia as in the past. But it does happen. This practice takes place in a number of instances. Sometimes the parents are against the marriage and the couple decides to elope. Sometimes the elopment is arranged with the parents' approval in order to avoid the tremendous wedding expense. Sometimes, "stealing the bride" can occur if the bride-to-be rejects the suitor.

An Abkhasian friend told me of his participation in an expedition to "steal the bride"—an honorable act, which he recounted with a gleam in his eye, to the obvious delight of the other Abkhasians present. The parents of the young woman refused to marry her to a suitor from a neighboring village. She was willing, however, and so they agreed that at a given signal she would leave her house through a window. The groom, as usual, had properly hidden himself, and a group of his friends was dispatched to bring her.

Meanwhile, the wedding feast was prepared and the guests assembled. Khachapuri were baked, bulls slaughtered, the chickens roasted to a beautiful glaze and ready to eat. But when the men on horseback arrived and gave the signal, the bride-to-be did not emerge from her house. Her parents had locked the door and boarded the windows. Reluctant to return without her, the young men waited discreetly in the mountain pass bordering the village. As they were about to leave, a messenger from the groom's family arrived, a very old man, respected and well known throughout the region. He went to every house in the bride's village where people of his own age lived, explained the situation, and asked for their help. Soon he had a committee of the eldest villagers, who went to plead with the reluctant parents.

"No one can refuse a group of the eldest people of their own village," my friend concluded, "and so we brought the bride home and the feast was on."

After the wedding, late at night, the groom steals his way into the *amhara* which is the bride's room or hut, built for the newlyweds, where they spend the nights during the first few weeks of married life. In former times, it was considered unmanly for a husband to exercise his sexual rights on the first night. However, some did, and in anticipation of it, his peers would surround the *amhara*, make noise, and even pull straw out of the structure in order to make a peephole. On that night the groom also removed the leather corset which the bride wore to make her small-waisted, and he cut off her chest band which was supposed to retard the development of her breasts.

Virginity is an absolute requirement for marriage. If a woman proves to have been previously deflowered, the groom has a perfect right to take her back to her family and his gifts must be returned. He always exercises that right, even at the present time. Announcing to the family, "Take your dead one," he leaves her in their house. Henceforth to him, as well as all other eligible men, she is dead. She has been so dishonored by his rejection that it would be next to impossible to find a man to marry her. Later on, however, she may be married off to an elderly widower or some other less desirable male from a distant village. When she is discovered, she is expected to name the guilty party, and she usually picks the

Old pre-Revolution house. On the left is the Amhara where the newlyweds spend the nights during the first few weeks of married life.

name of a man who has recently died, in order to prevent her family from taking revenge and beginning a blood feud.

If a woman stayed in the house of a strange man and he then refused to consider her his wife, she would be considered "spoiled." The same holds true for an engaged woman if the man should change his mind, though they were not living together. After the engagement and the official visit of the man's relatives to the woman's parents, they are considered legally married, and neither party can break the engagement without making bitter enemies of the rejected person's family.

Both the bride and groom remain hidden from their senior relatives after the wedding night. When the groom leaves the amhara (the Abkhasian word literally means "silent" or "not listening to"), he used to wear his headdress low on his face so that the old people could not recognize him. At present, instead of wearing a bashlick he wears a visored cap. If the husband is needed for work, he may be released in a couple of days and he comes to his father, to whom he offers a glass of wine. If the father accepts the wine, the young man is permitted to reveal himself. He also presents gifts to relatives, which are termed "ransom." This ransom is supposed to "cover the shame." It is still considered a polite gesture for a groom to be out of sight of the older relatives on his wedding night.

Traditionally, when a bride enters her husband's house, she receives a new name and, in return, gives new names to her brothers-in-law. This is a way perhaps of indicating that new relationships have been established between them. Presently, however, this custom is not observed strictly. For example, in the home of a very well respected elder in the village of Duripsh, the eldest daughter-in-law has changed her name while the youngest has not.

The expense of an Abkhasian wedding is tremendous. Because of many articles in the newspaper *Soviet Abkhasia*, and the condemnatory resolutions of the Komsomol, the weddings, as bounteous as ever, are often made for two brothers on the same day. In such cases, both brides stand in separate corners of the same room. Otherwise, weddings and funerals continue as they used to be in the villages, although they are simpler and less expensive in the cities.

Marriage Limitations   Although most Abkhasians have been Moslems for the last three hundred years, monogamy is still the rule. Marriage usually takes place between twenty and forty for a man and twenty to twenty-three for a woman. Earlier marriages, with rare exceptions, are not practiced. In 1966, in Atara, there were about fifty unmarried men, aged between twenty-five and forty. Among the women between thirty and forty, there were a large number of unmarried women. The population is kept down by late marriages and few children. According to all Abkhasian ethnographers, the marriage rules and taboos discussed in the last chapter retain their importance up to the present day.[3]

Consanguineal marriages are strictly prohibited. Members of the same family, regardless of the degree of remoteness, are forbidden to marry. Breaking this law is considered not only criminal, but provokes feelings of deep revulsion. In former times, incest was punished by death, usually at the hands of a near relative, such as a brother or a father. At the present time, a couple accused of incest is driven out of the village. Even people belonging to different nationalities, if by chance they carry the same or a similar name, cannot marry, since they would be considered descendants of the same progenitor. When I spoke to the young people of Duripsh about such marriages, their revulsion at the topic was apparent on their faces.

At the present time, the restrictions are relaxed in the third degree of the descending female line; that is, one may marry a person of the same surname as one's maternal grandmother. But this is still considered "not nice."

Affinal marriages, between a man and female relatives of his deceased wife or between a woman and male relatives of her deceased husband, are also prohibited. A man is expected to treat his wife's sister and her other close relatives as if he were their brother. Marriage with his wife's first cousin is considered undesirable. Equally undesirable are marriages of two brothers to two sisters, because the families are already related when the first brother marries. While marriage with members of the family of one's son- or daughter-in-law is prohibited, this does not extend to their entire lineages.

Ritual kinships also act as a barrier to marriage. For example, Moslem law prohibits marriage between the relatives of a woman and the man she wet-nursed. In the past, this prohibition extended not only to her blood and milk relatives, but also to the blood and milk relatives of her husband. Not long ago, marriage between a man's family and his wet nurse's entire lineage was taboo, but now the younger people would accept marriage with her second or third cousins, although the elders disapprove of such arrangements.

[3] L. E. Kuchberia, "On the Development of Marriage Customs and Wedding Rites among the Abkhasians," in *The Contemporary Abkhasian Village*. Tbilisi: Metznireba Publishers, 1967, p. 125.

Adoption, real or symbolic, involves the same prohibitions on marriage as does a consanguineal relationship. Islamic law considers adoption without nursing to be no obstacle to marriage, but Abkhasian custom equates both forms of adoption. Symbolic brotherhood is considered as real as consanguineal.[4]

Hamlets were originally settled by members of one lineage and, naturally, these people could not intermarry. But when some hamlets joined together into villages, the custom of local exogamy embraced the entire village.

In the past, even more trivial reasons existed to prohibit marriage. For instance, marriage to a friend who often visited the family and shared a meal with them was not looked upon with favor.

In addition to these rules, marriage is precluded by a number of physical defects: impotence, venereal disease, loss of mind, and deformities, especially congenital ones. Very little charity is displayed in appraising the physical characteristics of a potential mate.

A good example of settlement and marriage patterns is the village of Atara-Abkhaskaya, which, like a number of Abkhasian villages, is populated by members of one lineage, with a small sprinkling of outsiders.[5] This village of 265 homesteads is inhabited by the family Kvitsiniya, and a few other related families. Until very recent times, Atara was considered exogamous. Men of the Kvitsiniya line took wives from the villages of Kindgi, Dzhgerda and Chlou. The women took husbands from these villages. In this way, the families had dual connective bonds, which increased growth of their authority.

During the middle of the nineteenth century, a man named Butva came to the village of Atara. He married a woman from the family of Kvitsiniya, and had four sons. Further marriages between the two lineages were strictly forbidden. During the 1950s, a man of the Kvitsiniya line again married a Butva woman, and at the meeting of "honorable old men" was forced to admit this accomplished fact. When relating this, a well-known Abkhasian storyteller named Seilach Butva said that he feels embarrassed and ashamed every time he passes his parents' graves.

Marriages between Abkhasians and members of other nationalities were permitted but infrequent. In mixed marriages, the Abkhasian language is spoken, and children are brought up as Abkhasians. An Abkhasian man may marry a Georgian or Russian woman, but Abkhasian women seldom marry outsiders.

THE POSITION OF WOMEN

A woman's position in Abkhasian society is ambiguous. According to tradition, she is expected to be meek and obedient to the elders of her household, and she must not speak in the presence of senior relatives. She may participate in family rituals only after she is "clean," which means after menopause. Yet in the past, she

[4] L. J. Luzbetak thinks that families related by ritual friendships may have intermarried (*Marriage and the Family in the Caucasus*, Vienna, 1951). However, L. E. Kuchberia writes that *no* north Caucasian people except Ossetians were permitted to marry the relatives of their ritual brothers.

[5] Ts. N. Bzhaniya, "Family and Family Life in Abkhasian Collective Village," in *The Contemporary Abkhasian Village*. Tbilisi: Metzniereba Publishers, 1967.

also was expected to take up arms bravely when necessary, to fight alongside men, and to be stoic and relentless.

While women in Western nations have a greater degree of freedom, the Abkhasian woman enjoys greater respect. She has the respect and obedience of her children. Her relatives, especially her brother, are honored above her husband's relatives. Mother's milk is a symbol of purity and is sacred. According to popular belief, it possesses immense strength and can "burn" anyone who desecrates it. Flirtation, sexual relations, or even the thought of having sexual relations with someone who is in any way kin is an insult to mother's milk.

The Abkhasian woman need never fear physical or verbal assault from her husband or from any other man. It is considered vulgar to beat a woman or to insult her, although a woman who was beaten by her husband in former times could not use it as a reason for divorce. An insult to a woman of another lineage was cause for a blood feud. "If you love your mother," it is said, "don't insult the mother of other men."

However, this respect for women did not prevent Abkhasian men from exploiting their labor. For example, before the introduction of the water mill, women had to stay up during the night and grind corn on a stone, in addition to their other daily chores. During the harvest, they also went without sleep for long periods. An Abkhasian man called his wife "the one who feeds me." Nor did respect prevent men from enforcing customs which, even to the present day, prevent women from participating in decision-making in the village administration.

It is still considered inexcusable for a woman in the villages to extend a greeting to a man first, to sit with him at the same table, or even to talk to men who are her seniors. She may not join her husband when he is conversing with other people, or walk with him, or call him by name. Some of these traditions are simply a code of manners and, if the occasion calls for it, can be temporarily set aside.

For instance, custom forbids a married couple not only to demonstrate their affection in public, but even to sit next to each other. However, when I asked an old man and his wife to pose for a picture, he said, "Well, it is considered impolite in our society," but he put his arm around her and allowed the picture to be taken anyway.

Not infrequently, the Moslem mullahs register marriages according to the Shari'at and write a marriage certificate which always includes a clause divesting the woman of her right to talk. Some men, even if they are not believers, buy this certificate—which usually costs quite a bit of money—so that all those present will approve.

At one wedding in the village of Achandara, this certificate was displayed to the eight hundred guests present, after which the groom remarked to his friend, "You know, if you don't do what the others are doing, they think you are a nobody."

According to custom, girls and young women did not wear warm clothing. If it became very cold, another dress or shawl could be added. Older women could wear an open coat lined with a thin layer of wool or cotton. This custom was jealously defended even after the Revolution by husbands and mullahs, in order to keep the women from leaving the house. The custom has changed, but women are still prohibited from appearing in a gathering without kerchiefs covering their heads.

Women are always the last to wash their hands before a meal, the last to sit at the table, and the last to enter and leave a room. When there are no adult men present in the house, a small boy may sit down to eat with a guest, but a woman must not. She may not slaughter an animal for a meal until after she has ceased to menstruate, for meat from such an animal is considered unhealthy. (The word for ritual slaughter—done either by a man or an old woman—is different from the word for improper killing, which has a derogatory connotation.)

When a woman becomes pregnant, she conceals it as long as possible. It is considered unbecoming or immodest to speak about it, even to her own mother. Usually, she informs a friend who then tells her mother and mother-in-law. If these more experienced women wish to give her advice, it is passed on through a third person or mentioned in an offhand remark.

During labor, the woman used to return to her parents' home or go to the amhara, the separate building where she spent her wedding night. She was supposed to stay there for some time. To return to her husband too quickly was not considered proper. Both husband and wife were to show restraint at this time.

At present, everyone goes to the maternity clinic. Working women are entitled to fifty-six days of prenatal care and fifty-six days of postnatal care. During this time, women do not work but receive full pay.

As soon as childbearing begins, men must leave the house. A man may bring his wife to the hospital for treatment, except when she is in labor. Then he may not visit her, and relatives and neighbors must take her to the hospital.

It is considered shameful for a woman to cry out or to complain during childbirth, although she may cry at any injury. According to village doctors, anesthesia is used only in the most difficult cases and, at any rate, "women bear pain far better than men."

The village hospital in Duripsh was built in 1962, but before that a midwife and a visiting doctor attended to the needs of the populace. Although women are instructed in modern child care, they still feel that amulets play an important protective role.

In former times, the infant was born in a small conical structure in the courtyard. There a chicken was subsequently sacrificed and a prayer offered to the god of marriage, family, and the hearth. The birth of a child is now celebrated at a big feast, which it is believed all dead relatives attend. Food is prepared for them, in the hope that they will be placated and bring no harm to the infant. The family gathers in the big house, where chickens are sacrificed and special bread is baked. The mother gets on her knees and, holding a candle, wishes all good things to come for her baby. Afterwards, everyone sits down to eat. All present are supposed to partake of the sacrificial chicken along with bread and wine, to ward off any harm which might possibly befall the mother and child.

After bearing her first child, a woman returns to her parents' home, and there a ritual takes place to signal her separation from her parents' house. A prayer to the hearth spirit is pronounced: "Here we brought the sacrifice according to the custom of our fathers, and we ask you to permit our daughter to be separated from her family and to join another family. Give her your blessings." However, this ceremony does not free her from the duty of honoring her family days.

The status of a woman increases with age, parallel to that of a man. An old woman, after menopause, may slaughter animals and may participate in certain rituals which were formerly closed to her. If she has a reputation for cleverness, her advice may be sought. The high position of an old woman is confirmed in folklore. The story is told that among the race of dwarfs known as Atzans, there lived an old woman who had mothered some of the warriors, and who often gave them good advice. Once, when the Atzans were being pursued by their enemies and escape was cut off, she advised them to gather bread and salt and offer it to the enemy, who could not insult this offer of hospitality. They had to spare the Atzans, who otherwise would have been doomed to certain slaughter.

A young girl, living with her parents, has fewer obligations at home than do the daughters-in-law who have come to live with the family. She may go out when she pleases, and her chief concern is to take care of her beauty. After she marries, she starts at the bottom of the hierarchy, walking behind the senior daughters-in-law. Her status generally depends on the age of her husband rather than her own age relative to the other women. In the past, the youngest daughter-in-law did the most laborious chores, but at present, work is arranged to accommodate those who hold outside jobs, such as teachers or factory workers.

The oldest woman is in charge of the others, and is very much concerned with harmony in her domain. She has no interest in exacerbating difficulties between her children and their spouses, since her position is sacred in her son's heart, and no one can disturb this relationship. The daughters-in-law also prefer to maintain harmonious relationships. Since a woman cannot pick up her own child in front of senior relatives, the children in the family are alternately cared for by all the women, and mothers must rely on each other's goodwill.

According to ancient custom, a woman could not own or inherit property, either from her father or her husband. She only had control over her dowry. But she possessed the exclusive right of inheritance of the property of her deceased sister. According to custom the property of the dead woman—her personal clothing, her dowry—was passed on to her sisters. If there were no sister the property was passed on to her brothers, and only in the last resort, to her children. The husband was excluded from the possible inheritors. It was only in the last third of the 19th century, under the influence of Russian law, that the practice of willing the wife part of the husband's estate was established, and this occurred mainly in the upper class. Property was divided among a man's sons, and if he had no sons, among his male relatives in ascending and descending lines. The brothers or male relatives then assumed responsibility for supporting the young daughter or daughters and marrying them off. They were also responsible for the widow's welfare.

In the past, a man could divorce his wife if she did not love and honor his parents, relatives, and friends, or was not hospitable, or if she bore no children.

Now, if there is occasion for a divorce, the children remain in the father's home as members of his family. Occasionally, if they are very small, the mother takes them with her to her parents' home along with her dowry. The division of household belongings is always made on the basis of Abkhasian customary law, with the lion's share going to the husband. The house belongs to him, but if it was built during their marriage, her share of the goods increases.

After the divorce, all familial and blood ties between the respective families of the man and woman cease to exist. However, when a close relative of her ex-husband dies, she comes to the funeral with two or three other people, offers a brief lamentation, and leaves. If a divorced woman wishes to remarry, she can do so only from her parents' home. In this case, the wedding ceremony is very simple.

While the legal position of women in Abkhasia was drastically changed by the Soviet law to afford them equal rights and status with men, the rules are not as yet fully implemented. Women themselves sometimes slow the progress by keeping the customs "out of respect for the old people."

I had an opportunity to meet an outstanding young woman who was one of the leading workers in her collective and a village deputy. As we came in, my Abkhasian friend told me, jokingly, "Ask for the name of her husband." Not suspecting anything, I did so. She smiled and said, "You know very well that I am not supposed to pronounce his name." Nor did she ever speak in the presence of her father-in-law, even though he had given a large feast in her honor, in order publicly to give her permission to speak before him. After the feast, when questioned about her choice to remain silent in her father-in-law's presence, she said, "By doing this, I can show others that I honor him."

However, middle-aged women frequently express the hope and conviction that their children will not have to observe the prohibitions imposed on Abkhasian women by religion and customs.

At the present time it is mostly a matter of preference within a generation: the old people observe the customs but do not require their children to do so; the middle-aged are uncomfortable in breaking the rules, yet on occasion do so; the youths are free to observe or not to observe.

In the past, it was unthinkable for a woman to be head of the household, but this custom gradually began to change after the Revolution, and the change was accelerated by the Second World War. If the eldest male died, and his sons were in the army, his wife often assumed his position. Since Abkhasian men have an almost religious respect for their mothers, the sons would not attempt to dispute her when they returned. However, if she were timid and reluctant to take on such a responsibility, they, of course, stepped in. A good example is that of Olga Kvitsiniya, who became head of a family which included her three grown sons and their wives and children. The oldest son, after his return from the army, moved out of the "big house" into a separate dwelling. His share of the family possessions was decided on by his mother, who had assumed responsibility for all the important family decisions.

Some changes in the position of women are accepted with reluctance. A prominent Abkhasian intellectual of my acquaintance married a non-Abkhasian woman. She was university-educated and a long-time friend of the family. One morning after breakfast, she remained seated with her husband's eldest brother, conversing at the table. The husband said nothing, but the house soon was filled with a tremendous racket, as he opened and slammed the door.

"Why is my husband making such a noise?" the new bride asked her brother-in-law.

"Oh, you aren't supposed to speak to me any more," replied the older man.

She was amused and continued to behave as she had before the marriage. Since her husband was a modern man and a member of the Party, he knew that old customs must disappear in time, and he eventually accepted this less than traditional state of affairs. It is not unusual for Abkhasian intellectuals to be torn between the desire to live according to their progressive ideals and their deep attachment to national customs.

The transition to a collective economy and the drive for womens' rights has considerably changed the condition of women in Abkhasia so that now they work alongside men and some hold responsible positions in hospitals, schools, and offices. At home, however, the same division of labor prevails. Women have all their old obligations as well as a full-time job and are greatly overworked.

Men consider caring for the cattle, hunting, and plowing as their work. In addition to cooking and cleaning, women are in charge of domestic fowl and of the vegetable garden near their home, as well as having a primary obligation to raise the children.

In some families, with the agreement of the administration, women plant tobacco near their houses so that they can work for the collective and tend to their other chores as well. Women who have senior female in-laws are more fortunate since, although these women are authorities over them, they do share the housework that no male will touch even if there is only one woman in a large homestead.

Because the restriction on speech for women extends into middle age, women do not take part in discussions where senior relatives are present. They are not members of government bodies, even on collective farms where they may constitute the majority of the workers. Women teachers—the core of the Abkhasian rural intelligentsia—have difficulties continuing to work in their own locality, since they would have to speak with parents who may be senior relatives, Some, even if they manage to stay on the job, cannot speak at pedagogical meetings. After marriage, many women leave the Komsomol, and only a few enter the Communist Party. Often, married women experience difficulties in supervisory positions where it is necessary for them to talk to workers. In three collective farms where the majority of the workers were women, it was found that not one woman spoke at the general meetings, nor did any serve as members of the governing body.

In spite of the dual role of women, there are few complaints or attempts to change these attitudes. The changes that began after the Revolution and are continuing at present actually were made not because of women's rebellion and demands, but because women were assigned a new role which was approved by the elders.

SEX

The Abkhasians expect to live long and healthy lives. They feel that self-discipline is necessary to conserve their energies instead of grasping what sweetness is available to them at the moment.

The general opinion among Abkhasians is that regular sexual relations should start late in life because abstinence will prolong sexual potency and promote well-being. Postponement of satisfaction is not deemed frustrating but, rather, a hopeful expectation of future enjoyment. A continuation of sex life into old age is considered as natural as maintaining a healthy appetite or sound sleep. Abkhasians do not think that there is any reason why increased years should strip them of so human a function.

Among the aged, there are no bachelors or spinsters. Celibacy is regarded, to a certain extent, as abnormal, antisocial, and contrary to human nature. In one study, only one elderly spinster in the village of Shroma could be found. Very often, the old people give their good family life and late marriages as some of the reasons for their longevity. Many of the Abkhasian aged got married between the ages of forty and fifty, which was considered quite normal in former times, and stayed married for fifty, seventy, or even eighty years. There are quite a number of instances where both husband and wife are still alive, and often the husband is older by twenty to thirty years. At present, to the consternation of the elders, young people tend to marry in their middle twenties, instead of waiting until the more "proper" age of thirty.

A medical team investigating the sex life of the Abkhasians concluded that many men retain their sexual potency far above the age of seventy, and 13.6 percent of the women were found to continue menstruation after fifty-five years of age. Late menarchy and late menopause for women are both expressions of the same biological principle of the slow aging process. Biologically speaking, they are "late bloomers." Even young people appear to be many years younger than they actually are.

Kutzba Murat, aged one hundred one, confided in me that he waited to get married until sixty years of age "because I had a good time right and left" while he served in the Russian Army. At present, he said with a trace of sadness, "I have desire for my wife but no strength." One of his relatives married eight times and had nine children, the youngest of whom was born when he had reached one hundred. The doctors obtained sperm from him when he was one hundred nineteen, in 1963, and he still retained his libido and sexual potency.

However, there is an overwhelming feeling of uneasiness, shame, and even danger connected with any manifestation of sex in the presence of others. Extreme modesty is required at all times. This is as true for married people as it is for those unmarried. A woman may never change her dress or bathe in the presence of other people, nor may she expose her underarms, which are considered erogenous zones. When a wife is in a room with her husband, they keep their voices low so that no one will be able to hear them being together.

Despite the elaborate rules—perhaps, in part, because they are universally accepted—sex in Abkhasia is considered a good and pleasurable thing when it is strictly private. As difficult as it may be for the American mind to grasp, it is also guiltless. It is not repressed or sublimated into work, art, or religious-mystical passion. It is not an evil to be driven from one's thoughts. It is a pleasure to be regulated for the sake of one's health—like a good wine.

EMOTION AND ENDURANCE

The overt expression of emotionality is unacceptable to the Abkhasians, and this is apparent in their interpersonal relationships. They are expected to maintain control even under the greatest stress. However, the level of satisfaction is very high, and human relationships are of extraordinary intensity.

It is a point of pride to be able to master one's feelings. This is shown in many Abkhasian novels. There is a story about a father whose favorite son was killed by another man. The father was beside himself with grief. Yet when the killer came to ask forgiveness, with a sword hung around his neck and offering his own baby for adoption, the mother of the slain son took the baby in her arms and held it to her breast, legitimizing the adoption. No expressions of bitterness were permitted between them afterwards. It would be unusual, even remarkable, if the father should continue to feel bitterness in the context of this culture. And yet, in a sense, that father had his satisfaction; for in the presence of witnesses, he conquered his feelings and proved his strength as an Abkhasian man. Theoretically, he had the option to take the applicant's sword and cut off his head. Had he actually done so, he would have been universally despised.

While sexual relationships between people of the same family are forbidden, this does not cause a problem. The feelings are so well repressed that they remain unconscious. For instance, a young man who falls in love with a woman and finds out later on that she is distantly related to him, immediately loses sexual desire for her. A young couple who are forbidden by their families to marry may become brother and sister through the appropriate ritual, after which they have the right to hug and kiss each other. This mechanism provides a satisfactory outlet for passion rather than exacerbating it.

Physical endurance is just as important as emotional control. If a man has to leave the table to relieve himself during a feast, he is not supposed to return. A woman may go out, because she never sits down anyway, and no one knows where she is going. But a man who cannot stand the pressure of his bladder is considered unmanly.

Friendships are cemented by extending the kin bond, through ritual brotherhood. They are of great intensity, and it is said, "For two friends, even a single plank is bed enough." A story is told of two friends who went to court. One had to defend his case before the populace. As he was speaking, he thrust the sharp end of his staff into the ground to emphasize his point; but this time he missed the ground and penetrated his friend's foot. The friend kept quiet, not wishing to interrupt the speech. At the end, when the first man pulled his staff up, blood gushed out of his friend's boot.

"Why didn't you tell me?" asked the man.

"But that was such an important speech," his friend replied. "I didn't want you to lose your train of thought."

The Abkhasians react to emotional adversity by directing their energies outward, rather than brooding or becoming depressed. Insults are to be avenged. Grief at funerals is often given violent, though ritualized, expression. Aggression is expressed overtly, and people are not secretive about their feelings. Black magic is rarely practiced.

The Abkhasian concept of endurance differs from the Oriental concept of passive acceptance. It involves struggling against unpleasant circumstances while enduring hardships. The people are not introspective, and suicide is rare.

The stoicism of the Abkhasians originated in the far past, when the consciousness of the people was permeated with the spirit of the warrior. The first task of every generation was the rearing of courageous and enduring sons. Bravery is the *sine qua non* of a man, and it is said that, "Cowards never have good luck."

FUNERALS

The one occasion when outbursts of feeling are permitted is at a funeral. As the Abkhasians see it, their system is rational, but death is, of its very nature, irrational and unjust. At such times, one is permitted to rage, to express one's grief by wailing and scratching at one's flesh. But even the expression of sorrow must be done according to rules. It is said that "A man who can't cry will break his head open with his fists."

An Abkhasian must be buried as soon as possible after his death. When a man or woman dies, all the relatives and neighbors are notified, by messenger on horseback (usually a neighbor, who is called "the one who carries the grief to the people") or by telephone and telegraph. Delegates may fly home from Moscow for the funeral.

It is the customary duty of the neighbors to build the coffin, dig the grave, prepare and serve food for the guests, and contribute to the funeral expenses. "Neighbors" in Abkhasia are not only those who live close to the house of the deceased, but include households that are some distance away. My Abkhasian colleague's mother counted forty homesteads as her neighbors. Thus at some funerals, the neighbors may number several hundred.

A large canopy is erected in the courtyard, the coffin placed underneath it, and benches set on three sides. Women are buried ten centimeters deeper than men. Men approaching the coffin must place their hats and any weapons they may be carrying on a nearby table. Women must leave their bags and umbrellas on a table at which a special attendant stands. There are a number of attendants present, as well as a director of services, to make sure that the funeral, or *kelekhi-ainykhra*, is performed with decorum, dignity, and order.

A mourner is not permitted to cry as he stands by the coffin, for fear that a tear may drop upon the body. Should that occur, those tears which touched the body will form a lake in the next world, which will separate the deceased from his relatives. The spouse, parent or child of the deceased may not show grief at all; but everyone else cries and yells, scratches his cheeks and forehead. The women in particular may scratch their cheeks until blood flows. The female relatives sit behind the coffin, many with their hair unbound, periodically crying, "aow," a word denoting grief. The people all try to wear black to the funeral, and the dead man's horse, which stands in the courtyard, is also draped in black. After everyone

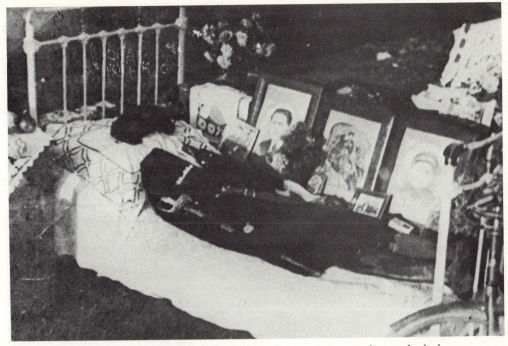

Mourning ritual for a deceased man. His traditional costume is spread over the bed.

has paid his respects, the people lead the horse around the courtyard three times. Then the deceased is buried, sometimes in the courtyard, sometimes in the cemetery belonging to the lineage or the entire settlement.

At such a funeral, I observed that, though the expression of grief is real and intense, as soon as the mourners walk away from the coffin and take their hats, bags and weapons, they cease to cry. Even grief is well-regulated in Abkhasian society.

Subsequently, the close relatives must wear black for forty days, and they may not eat meat or milk. The maternal uncle, or closest relative of that line, provides a suit of clothes called the anshan, which rests on the bed of the deceased during the first forty days after his death; and friends and relatives come by to cry in front of it. Memorial services are conducted on the fortieth day, the fifty-second day, and the first anniversary. These are similar to the funeral, except that the corpse is replaced by the suit of clothes, and the horse stands by it during the service.

There are no village cemeteries. Christians and Moslems are buried side by side, at some place that they are particularly fond of, or on their own property.

In the past, Abkhasians used to have sharpshooting contests and displays of horsemanship at funerals. This custom has disappeared, but they still hold huge processions, with hundreds of relatives who must be fed. It is the neighbors' obligation to bring a large dish of nuts, and the wives prepare *fasola* (beans with crushed walnuts). Speeches are made, and large quantities of wine are consumed.

This practice, which may be financially ruinous for a family, has been condemned by the Abkhasian Party leadership; but Abkhasian Communists still attend the same weddings and funerals which they deplore. They show a considerable sense of humor about the situation, as can be seen in these excerpts from a local newspaper:

> The readers . . . surely remember a letter from the Secretary of the Communist Party organization in the village of Apsny, which appeared on these pages. In this letter, the author convincingly demonstrated the socially destructive nature and financial waste of the funeral rituals. . . .
>
> Representatives of the worker's committees, the intellectuals, the Komsomol— indeed everyone [in Abkhasia] was very enthusiastic and entirely in agreement. . . . But the reality of the situation turned out to be quite different from our expectations. . . .
>
> In the village of Dranda, the mother of a political instructor passed away. We would assume that the instructor of the Communist committee should know better; but he himself could not resist temptation, nor could he convince his father not to throw an elaborate funeral. . . .
>
> . . . Even the chairman of the Communist committee of Dranda took an active part. . . . When the chairman of the collective farm . . . saw us coming, he became very embarrassed and looked at the long tables as though he were seeing them for the first time. "When did they have the time to make it all?" he asked innocently.[6]

The author of this article cites a number of similar occurrences, of funerals attended by hundreds of mourners, and the "disgraceful amount of drinking which takes place at these ceremonies." Most of the individuals whom he singles out are Party members. However, tradition provides the main social entertainment, marks the high points in the individual's life and reaffirms one's unity with the lineage. It will be some time before these customs can be replaced.

[6] A. Avidzba, "Let's Wipe Out Obsolete Rituals: Again the Kelekhi-Ainykhra," *Soviet Abkhasia*, June 15, 1970.

6/Religion and folklore

ISLAM AND CHRISTIANITY

It has been said that the Abkhasians are pagans, Moslems, Christians and even atheists simultaneously. The Abkhasian pantheon is full of deities and spirits. But neither orthodox Christianity, which came from Byzantium during the fifth century, in the reign of the Emperor Justinian, nor the Sunni sect of Islam, which was introduced by the Turks during the fifteenth and sixteenth centuries, could erase pagan beliefs connected with the lineage and family structure. The spread of Islam was facilitated by strong family ties, especially along female lines, between Abkhasians living in Turkey and those remaining in their own land.

The year 523 A.D. is given as the date of the official establishment of Christianity, but this religion never took real roots, although the Russians later attempted to superimpose it on the people with great force. The Turks, equally conscientiously and with equal force, tried to establish Islam, but the adherents of each religion whom I encountered had little understanding of religious dogma.

The peasants embraced Islam selectively, ignoring some ritual abstinences, such as wine, but observing such holidays as Ramadan and Kurban Bairam, and following Moslem rites of burial and circumcision. They celebrate Easter, distinguishing two Easter Sundays—the first for men and the next for women.

In the past, the best cow in every Abkhasian household, regardless of religious affiliation, was selected and dedicated to St. George. This was done by cutting off a piece of her ear. If she had a bull calf, he was sacrificed to the saint; but if she bore a heifer, the sacrifice was made with a lamb.[1] At the present time, even members of the Communist Party, some with considerable education, still participate in family rituals and holidays.

Exact percentages of people belonging to certain faiths are not known and can not easily be obtained. Most Abkhasians do not define themselves in terms of a select religion.

A survey of religious practices, however, was made in the village of Duripsh. Five percent of the people of Duripsh are Orthodox Christians, and 85 percent are Moslems. Only 5 percent of the Moslems are "pure Moslems." These have a high percentage of illiteracy and believe that the earth is flat, resting on the horns

---

[1] S. T. Zvanba, *Ethnographic Studies*. Sukhumi: Alashara, 1955, p. 56.

of a huge black bull, who in turn stands on the head of an enormous fish.[2] For this reason, Abkhasians always remove the head of a fish before eating it.

Of the rest of the Moslems, 32 percent are not particularly religious, though Islamic beliefs are projected into their *Weltanschauung*. The remaining 63 percent are not considered religious at all. However, when G. V. Smyr lectured to them to prove that there was no God, he made such a good impression that they gratefully gave him their amulets in order to protect him from evil spirits. No less than 50 percent of the population still observe Moslem holidays. People who declare that they have religious beliefs are usually above forty, and women are usually more religious than men.

The holiday which is most widely celebrated in Abkhasia is the thirty-day Moslem fast called Uraza (Ramadan), when people may not eat from the appearance of the sun until sunset, and married couples sleep separately. Out of 655 people interviewed, 287 kept the fast, either personally or with their families. It is believed that during this period, the dead relatives can see and hear their surviving kin, and they also live an earthly life. Food is laid out for the recently deceased.

Another widespread holiday is Kurban Bairam, the day of sacrifices, on which almost every family tries to sacrifice its best sheep. This is supposed to help people cross the bridge to heaven.

The prohibitions on speech for women are widespread in the Caucasus and are not peculiarly Abkhasian or Moslem. The Muslim dictate that young people should not meet alone was taken seriously until quite recently. On the whole, only those dictates which reinforced preexisting customs were adopted.

The main local spirits who receive respect from adherents of all religions are: Ufa, who rules the thunder and all atmospheric changes; Shasta, protector spirit and ruler of blacksmiths and all the arts; Azhvenshaa, the spirit of the forest, wild animals and hunting; and Aitar, the protector of domestic animals. The supreme being is called Amtzva, the plural form of the word for mother.

The fact that the Greek Orthodox Church and the Moslem mullahs were little interested in the form in which the Abkhasians adopted Christianity or Islam resulted in the development through centuries of a peculiar mosaic of fragments of religious beliefs. Christian ceremonies, Moslem rites and pagan observances are so closely interwoven that at times it seems almost impossible to separate them.

The following response was elicited from a twenty-five-year-old woman, in answer to the question, "What does God look like?"

"He is rather small in size, gray-haired, has children, never was sick, and his parents are buried in heaven."

LINEAGE AND FAMILY CULTS

While riding along with an Abkhasian friend, I remarked on the beauty of a mountain in the distance. "Ah, yes," he said, "that is Branba's mountain. But our sacred mountain is more beautiful."

[2] G. V. Smyr, *Islam in Abkhasia.* Tbilisi: Metzniereba, 1972, p. 15.

"What do you mean?" I asked. "Do you own the mountains?"

"Each lineage has its own sacred place," he replied. "We gather there once a year and pray; we make sacrifices and discuss the problems of various members. That mountain belongs to the Branba lineage. Ours is quite a distance from here and, as I said, it's more beautiful."

Most, if not all, of the religious practices of Abkhasia are rituals which reinforce the family structure. For this reason, even those who are not religious participate in them. They give a sense of unity and collective responsibility. At the same time, since each lineage has its own sacred place and protective spirits, the Abkhasian attitude towards religion is tolerance. Religion is a family matter, and inquiries are not made into the beliefs of strangers.

The mountain of Kulanyrkhva is sacred to the lineage of Gumba. At this place, a bull is usually sacrificed at the yearly assemblage. The animal is contributed by each abipara in turn, or bought collectively.

Soviet investigators think that the earliest form of religion in Abkhasia was totemism. The lineage Tzugba consider themselves related to the cat (atzgu). The Kishba lineage believe that the jay is a relation. They cannot kill this bird or use its meat, for "how can you kill a namesake?" Kishba means literally, sons or descendants of the bear, and Branba, sons of the wolf.

Every lineage observes at least one day in a week called amash-shar, the forbidden day when certain types of work may not be performed. Families have different days and different prohibitions. For example, men of the Ashuba line are not allowed to sell or lend anything from the house on those days, and women may not spin or sew. The family Gerzmava cannot kill or eat rabbits on certain days. Certain occupations have restrictive days; for example, days on which hunters may not trap martens.

Family cults are inherited through the father. A married woman must observe the rituals of her father's cult as well as her husband's, and this may be quite inconvenient for the household.

Certain rituals can only be performed by men, others by women, and still others by men only, but with women present. The old deities connected with agriculture are female: Dzhadzha, deity of fields, grapes and vegetable gardens; and Anapa-haga, deity in charge of fertility of the land. In the past, only a woman past menopause could pray to Dzhadzha. But when agriculture became economically important in Abkhasia, men supervised the cash crops and eventually, towards the end of the nineteenth century, took over the prayers.

During the nineteenth and early twentieth centuries, if a long dry spell occurred, the whole community would arrange a prayer for rain. They would invite the most honorable or the oldest man, who would speak with God to convince Him that the rain should fall on the village. Quite a bit of oratory was used.

One such speech was recorded:

You can see the people here, men and women, how hard they worked on your earth, to sow and improve it. The sun burnt them, and they were thirsty, and now our success hangs on the rain. The earth is thirsty. If there is no rain, there will be no harvest, and the people will not work, and the earth will be barren.

The eldest male of the Azhvala with a glass of wine in his right hand prays for the good life for members of his Azhvala.

The old protectors of the hunt, Airg and Azhveipshaa, were male deities and they had dominion over the woods and forest animals. In the *Nart* epics, about the legendary forefathers of the Abkhasians, hunting was one of the chief economic occupations of the heroes. All of the Narts were outstanding hunters, and they were always accompanied by large numbers of wolves, who served them as dogs. Sasrykva, the central figure of the epics, is called the "Top Hunter" and he is the ruler of the game. He is always accompanied by his dog Khudish.

The hunters used a secret language known only to themselves, so the animals would not know what they were talking about. This "language of the woods" was shared with other Caucasian peoples, though each group had its own ordinary language. The eldest hunter in the group is called the "Lucky Bull"; generally, the leader of a group of shepherds in the alpine meadows is called by this name in the Caucasian region.

During the hunt, the hunters and their families once had to observe certain religious and magical rites in order to appease the protectors and the animals. For instance, before leaving the house, the hunter usually took some personal effect from each relative and guest and even each dog, and burnt it in the fire. It could be something so insignificant as the hair of a dog. He then said, "If there is a quarrel in my household or any ill fortune during my absence, let this not disturb my hunt." The people at home were not supposed to talk about the hunters, or mention where they were going, so that they could catch the animals by surprise. They were careful not to have any disagreements or to use any words which might be considered improper, so that they would not offend the protector spirits.

According to the rules of hunting, past and present, the animal belongs to the man whose arrow or bullet first touches it, not to the one who kills it ("the law of the first blood"). The moment he hits the animal, he begins to sing a song to the protector of the woods, and this is a signal to the other hunters, who come running. After the kill the hunter cuts off a piece of the ear and nose, and throws these away. Then the animal belongs to the hunter, and not to the protector spirits.

Coming home from a good hunt, the hunter begins to sing to let people know he is coming. Everyone comes out to greet him, singing "To whom you gave, you are going to give again." The hunter sings a special song in praise of the protector spirits.

Besides hunting, pastoralism has been an important part of the Abkhasian economy since earliest times, and has a very important place in religious beliefs and epic songs. One of the most honored pagan deities was Aitar, protector of domestic animals. Until the twentieth century, it was customary to take one hundred lambs and kids out of the herds annually and set them free in the woods. This was the portion belonging to Ashveipshaa, and presumably they were devoured by wolves and other wild animals. If they came out of the woods and returned to their owner, this was considered a bad omen, for his hospitality had been rejected.

MUSIC

Many visitors have remarked on the importance of song, music, and dance in Abkhasia. There are songs for all occasions: joyous songs for weddings, ritual

Rodon Gumba, composer, writing down the storytelling of Makhty Tarkil.

songs, cult songs, lullabies, healing songs, and work songs. There are special songs for the gathering of the lineage, for a dancing bear, for someone who has measles or St. Vitus' dance; songs celebrating the exploits of heroes, or historical and revolutionary events; humorous songs and contemporary ones. It is believed that hunters must sing their song before leaving for a hunt, or they will not catch anything. The favorite songs reflect the Abkhasian admiration for heroes.

The Abkhasians' favorite instrument is the apkhartsa, which resembles a two-stringed dulcimer, and is played with a bow.[3] A player accompanies himself with song, and listeners join in. Both men and women know how to play and sing, but only men can perform in public, since women's voices may not be heard by their senior male relatives. In former times, every village had a few outstanding players, who were very much admired.

According to the old people, the apkhartsa was widely used in battle. People still believe that its music has a psychological effect.[4] The player used to march in front of his comrades, and if he fell, another man took his instrument and began to play. The word *apkhya* from which the name of the instrument is derived means "forward" in Abkhasian. Songs were often composed and played while enemies were besieging villages, in order to hearten the defenders. They praised those who died in combat and celebrated historical events. Some of these were very sad, expressing grief over the Abkhasians who suffered under Turkish rule.

[3] I. M. Kashba, "Musical Culture of the Abkhasians", in *The Contemporary Abkhasian Village*. Tbilisi: Metzniereba Publishers, 1967.

[4] Dr. Walter C. McKain reports that Soviet scientists are currently experimenting with music therapy in various "zones of health" established by Dr. Sh. M. Gusanov. W. C. McKain, "The Zone of Health," *The Gerontologist, 9*, No. 1, 1969.

Music from the apkhartsa supposedly alleviates pain. A story is told of a man named Kuchuk, who had to have a bullet removed from his leg. During the operation, he played on his apkhartsa, and showed no signs of suffering. His wife, who was standing nearby, let him know in a roundabout way that it was not fitting for a real man to try to alleviate pain in this way. He immediately stopped playing and kept silent until the end of the operation.

The Abkhasians have a few songs for wounded people. One is sung during the operation, the next afterwards, and another, called "The Song of the Wounded One" is sung by friends and relatives to help him get well. Sometimes the injured person may sing to himself. This music is considered sacred.

Songs are used like medicine. When someone takes sick, his relatives, in addition to assuming his responsibilities, surround his bed during the night and tell him jokes and stories and sing and dance, in order to take his thoughts away from the pain.

When a man is about to die, relatives sing quietly and play at his bedside, and also at his memorial services. Although a father cannot cry at his son's death, he can express his feelings in song.

FOLKLORE

The folklore of Abkhasia, particularly the Nart epics and the stories about Abrskil, the Abkhasian Prometheus, shows strong parallels with that of other peoples of the Caucasus. The Nart epics hold a very important place in North Caucasian, and to some extent in Transcaucasian, folklore. They indicate the world view of the people, and make interesting comments on interpersonal relationships. In the opinion of Soviet ethnographers, the Nart epics probably were formed over a period of 2000 years, beginning in Scythian times (800–700 B.C.), and continuing up to the Tatar-Mongolian invasions of the thirteenth century.[5]

According to some legends, the Atzans, a race of midgets, were forerunners of the giant Narts. According to others, they were contemporaries, and had close and peaceful relations. They hunted on the same ground and, according to the mountain customs, they shared their kill.[6] They were so small that they could easily walk along the stem of a fern and cut off the branches as they went. In spite of their size, the Atzans were wide-chested and broad-shouldered. They displayed great physical power, bravery, and courage. Anyone of them could, for example, while on the hunt, lift onto his shoulders and carry to camp his killed game— aurochs and mountain goat. In addition they were unsurpassed runners.

The Atzans basically lived by hunting and herding. They began breeding a special variety of long-bearded goats. However, they also cultivated wheat. Both goats and wheat are said by the Abkhasians to be the gifts of the Atzans to mankind.

[5] Y. S. Smirnova, "Military Democracy in the Epic Narts," *Soviet Ethnography*, Academy of Sciences of the USSR, 6, 1959.
[6] Sh. D. Inal-Ipa, *Pages of Abkhasian Historical Ethnography*. Sukhumi: Alashara, 1971.

With their cattle the Atzans spent most of their time under the open sky, in huts of wild rushes, or in their small stone shelters where they also kept their cattle. The small stone enclosures which are commonly seen in the mountains of Abkhasia are still attributed to the Atzans. Nothing disturbed them—neither heat nor cold, neither rain nor snow. And they recognized no authority over them except that of the tribe elder—"the great father of the Atzans." But they were good, honest little people. Proud and freedom-loving, they did not tolerate condescension, demanding equality in their dealings with others.

The Atzans' downfall is told as follows:

Once, when the Atzans were seated in their "fence-fortress," a miraculous child in a golden cradle or chariot unexpectedly descended from the skies. The good people took him in as a milk brother with joy and tenderness. Thus, the Atzans became related to God himself unintentionally, as the foster parents of his nephew or son. The child grew to be a fine young man of normal size. Time passed, and he left his foster parents and returned to the skies.

Gradually their unrestricted freedom made the Atzans conceited, dishonest, and uncontrollable. They began to deny the existence of any authority, even God.

"Who is God? Above us—the sky, and below the sky, we are," they said.

The Atzans became unclean creatures, defiling their water sources. The turbulent waters dried up and disappeared when they settled on the shores. They began turning their faces mockingly to the skies when urinating. For amusement they began to use their wooden barrels, in which they kept sour milk, for shooting targets.

All of this did not please God, and there was no limit to his anger. "I will show them what it means to not heed Me," he thought, and he decided to punish the Atzans for their sacrilege and lack of faith. However, he did not know how best to do this. So he called his nephew (son) to him, who was brought up by the Atzans, and entrusted him with the task of finding out the best way of annihilating them.

The messenger of God arrived among the Atzans, who were gathered in a circle in their stone shelter. The youth, addressing the elder, asked:

"Tell me, you are so small but not afraid of anything. Is there any force that can overcome you?"

To this they answered:

"There is only one means of conquering us, and that is fire. If dry cotton covers the entire earth like deep snow, and if there falls on it a spark which flames up and burns the entire world, then this can destroy us. Nothing else do we fear."

Having heard this, the youth vanished.

Some time passed. One day, the three hundred-year-old father of the Atzans, sitting in the shade with his herd, was resting. He was sitting in the shade of the long beard of a goat, so you can imagine what the goat was like and what kind of beard he had. All of a sudden he noticed that the usually unmoving goat beard, which reached the ground, suddenly began to tremble strangely. This was the wind which God was sending to the earth. A horrible fear seized the wise old man, and all of the Atzans felt that something disastrous was about to happen.

"My children!" cried the old man, "it seems as if we brought up that young boy in vain. We adopted him as our own and he betrayed us. But there is nothing we can do—our end has come!" Thus spoke the old man, addressing his fellow tribesmen and pointing to the goat whose beard was trembling more and more from the rising wind.

"This wind presages nothing good, nothing good. . . ."

The wind became more and more powerful. It drove before it black clouds, which covered the sun. From behind the clouds white clumps of cotton began to fall onto the earth. Then thunder roared and lightning flashed. The sparks from the lightning set the cotton afire, and in a moment everything had burned to ashes.

And so the Atzans perished. They suffered this horrible fate because of their insolence and pride.

It is important to note that in all the vast folklore about the Atzans no names or personalities are emphasized—the only one that stands out from the rest is that of the elder. This is in marked contrast to folklore about the Narts where many characters display individualistic traits. In addition, all of the Atzans' activities— herding, hunting, planting, and harvesting—was done in groups. This testifies to a strong spirit of collectivism and community among the Atzans, according to Inal-Ipa.[7]

Of all the legends of Abkhasia, the Atzans' is perhaps the only one in which a divine being deceives people and destroys them; it also is the only fatalistic legend. Like the local Promethean legends, it may possibly have been influenced by the Greeks. However, Greek deities led people to commit crimes, such as incest or *hubris*, before destroying them. In this case, the Atzans committed no crimes but rather showed hospitality and trust.

The main occupation of the Narts, a tribe of heroes, was war, and the most honorable occupation was that of a warrior. The blacksmith's trade, and the art of metallurgy, were also surrounded with glory.

> The Narts were courageous and strong,
> Their power was glorified in song,
> And they spent all their time at war.

The Nart epics are filled with the ideals of a warrior people, unending tales of military expeditions to "earn glory," hunts, feasts, and martial games. The goal of war was to plunder, to steal cattle and other treasures. At the same time, occasional stories are told about the defense of the homeland. Smirnova thinks that the Narts were a group of warriors distinguished from the rest of the population during the period of "military democracy" (comparable to Greek society during Homer's *Iliad*).[8] She feels that the Nart epics are even more democratic because they reflect the idea of a forthcoming victory of the peasants.

The Narts were the hundred sons of the same mother, Satani-Guasha. They had a sister, whom they honored by giving her only the bone marrow of the best game to eat.

One day, while bleaching the material which she had just spun on the bank of a river, Satani-Guasha was overcome by the heat of the day and decided to take her clothes off and cool herself in the waters. She was floating naked on her back

[7] Inal-Ipa, 1965, p. 597.
[8] Smirnova, 1959.

when she noticed Zartyzh, the shepherd who served her sons, standing on the opposite bank while his bulls grazed nearby. She called to him and asked him to swim over to her. Overcome by her beauty, he jumped into the river and tried to swim across, but was thrown back by the strong currents. He tried three times but each time he was thrown back. Finally, in desperation, he called to her and said:

"I can't make it. Get out of the water and stand next to the boulder. I will direct my arrow to it and you will conceive; but you must ask Ainar, the blacksmith, to come here and give you the image from the boulder where the arrow strikes it. Later the child will be born to you."

She did as she was directed, and twelve months later, she had a son, whom she named Sasrykva. He was also called, "not the real Nart," because he was illegitimate.

Satani-Guasha was noted for her great beauty and everlasting youth, as well as her wisdom. She ranked higher than her husband, who had become an old and decrepit man and sat by the fire all day. Her ninety-nine sons worshiped her for her beauty, her great skill as a mother and as a housewife. When they returned from a prolonged expedition and found her with the new baby, they demanded to know who the father was, well aware that their own father was past the age of paternity. She told them it was a supernatural birth and would not reveal any of the details. However, Sasrykva later forced her to tell him the actual facts.

There was great rivalry between Sasrykva and his ninety-nine brothers, because he wanted to be accepted as an equal and liked by his brothers, but they resented him, saying, "You were not born legally. Your father was unknown and you aren't our brother." In addition, he was a superhero, and they could not abide this.

Sasrykva accomplished all kinds of impossible feats from the day of his birth. Ainar, the blacksmith, held him by one leg and dipped him into a cauldron of hot steel, then poured some down his throat. The only part of him which was untouched by steel was the leg which had been held. Therefore, it was thought that (like the Greek Achilles) he was immune to all dangers. His brothers finally killed him by challenging him to use his untreated leg to kick a large boulder. In doing this, he broke his leg and died.

In addition to the war exploits, a great many epics describe the armor, spears and arrows of the warriors. Ainar the blacksmith is presented as a clever and strong man. His right hand is a hammer, his left is a pair of tongs, and he uses his left leg as an anvil.

Once Sasrykva, who was hunting in the woods, saw one of the little Atzans next to a bull. The bull was so large that this dwarf could hardly be seen next to his kill. The little Atzan offered to share his catch, saying, "Give me my part, and the rest is yours."

"No," said the cunning Sasrykva, "You take as much as you can carry, and the rest will be enough for me." And he thought, "How much can you carry, little man?" However, the Atzan understood his trick, and he tied up the legs of the bull, put the rope to his shoulder and quietly walked off. Sasrykva was left empty-handed.

The same story is told about another Nart named Kun. He followed the Atzan home, and there saw the dwarf's sister, a woman named Zylka. She was spinning so industriously that the houses in the settlement shook. Kun was taken with her and wanted to marry her, but the Atzans were reluctant. They did not want their sister, from a tribe of simple folk, to go to the home of the proud Narts, who might insult her. Kun swore that he would always respect her. Zylka said that she would like to marry him, but if he ever did insult her for her small size, she would leave him immediately.

A hundred bulls were slaughtered for the wedding feast. As a good wife, Zylka did not come out of the wedding hut right after the marriage, but she sewed the hides of the slain bulls into a ball and threw it out the window. The Narts played with it, bouncing it so high that it finally touched the clouds.

Once, Kun was going to race horses with the others, but he noticed that his riding boot was torn. Zylka had not noticed it. "Woe is me," he complained, "that's what comes of marrying a dwarf woman." She overheard him, went into the house, and cut her belly open with a knife. Then she removed a child and threw it out the window. "That's all I have in common with you people," she said, and walked out, returning to her family.

Kun and the other Narts were very upset. The baby lay in the middle of the grass, but no nurse could get near him, for he was hot as a blacksmith's furnace. Finally, the family sent word to Zylka and asked her what to do. She said that the boy should be fed liquid iron, and indeed he seemed to thrive on it. They named him Tzvitzv.

He was expected to become a hero, but all he did was sit by the fire and whittle. In actuality, he was more cunning, heroic, modest and noble than all the other Narts. He disguised himself and his horses when he went out to do battle, painting his horses half white and half black. One day the Narts were about to divide their plunder, and he asked for his share.

"What did you do to earn it?" they inquired.

"The water will tell the truth," he said. So they set out cauldrons of water, and as he enumerated his deeds, his cauldron boiled over. In that way, they knew he was telling the truth, and Sasrykva embraced him.

Eventually the Narts died out, and the people were sad. One of the cleverest of the people said, "We have so much wealth. Why don't we kill some of the animals, come together and eat them? Then it will be easier to stand the loss."

On a given day, all the people came together, and some were chosen to prepare the feast. Others had to capture the Narts' horses, and they covered the horses with special funeral blankets called atarche'em. Only Sasrykva's horse could not be captured. Those who prepared the food worked very hard, but the others just sat and mused about the Narts. They became bored and finally decided to arrange horse races and archery competitions, and those who were best would receive prizes. They sang the horse-racing song. The festivities lasted for seven days.

One day a traveler, a virtuous man, was returning home. Night fell, and he had to sleep in the forest. As soon as he fell asleep, somebody yelled out the name of Sasrykva, and then "Come here with the guest, we'll eat!" Then Sasrykva came to him, and led him to the place where the Narts were seated at their tables, each •

of which was covered with food. Only Sasrykva's table was empty. When the guest arrived, each of the Narts brought a little food to Sasrykva's table. He explained to his guest:

"When we all died, our neighbors spent all we had in our memorial services. But because my horse was not captured and did not take part in the races, I was left without my part of the funeral feast. My horse is called Bzoy, and he eats steel. The spot on which you sleep is my grave."

The traveler, upon awakening, went to the village of the Narts, and called everyone to a meeting. He told them what he had seen. They decided to make a memorial service for Sasrykva, but because so little remained of the Narts' wealth, they brought their own animals to be slaughtered. Everyone, including the traveler, gave what he could, and arranged a beautiful memorial. The traveler caught Sasrykva's horse, covered it with the funeral blanket, and later rode off on it. Before the people dispersed, they decided that whenever someone died, all the relatives and neighbors must make a big feast and arrange horse races. They must sing only the horse-racing song at funeral feasts, and they must not dance.

Throughout the tales, most of Sasrykva's troubles were caused by his illegitimacy. Legitimacy is traced through the father, and the children belong to his lineage if he and his wife should divorce. There are no half-brothers in Abkhasia. In general, the tales reinforce the Abkhasian world view and family structure.

In many European stories, the mother-in-law is portrayed as being cruel to her daughter-in-law. In Abkhasian folklore, the reverse is the case: a bad daughter-in-law is seen as trying to harm her mother-in-law. In one story, the younger woman tried various means of creating difficulties between her husband and his mother. The young man noticed her manipulations, but kept quiet.

Her favorite trick was to put extra salt in the dish which she placed in front of her mother-in-law, with a little mark on the dish so she could recognize it. The old woman never said a word in complaint, but she was always thirsty.

One day, the husband decided to teach his wife a lesson. He switched the dishes when her back was turned, so she had to eat up the salty food which she had prepared. Before retiring, he poured out the water which had been set aside for drinking during the night.

The young woman woke up terribly thirsty, and had to go out to the stream for a drink. Her husband quietly followed her. As she went on her knees and bent her head to drink, he sneaked up behind her and pushed her up and down a few times, until she lost consciousness. Then he went home quietly, leaving her on the bank. After she revived, she came home and told her husband that a spirit had punished her for mistreating his mother. And she never did it again.

7 / Why Abkhasians are long-living

My studies carried out in Abkhasia have led me to believe that Abkhasians live as long as they do primarily because of the cultural, social, and psychological factors that structure their existence. The most important are: the uniformity and predictability of both individual and group behavior, the unbroken continuum of life's activities, and integration of the aged into the extended family and community life as fully functioning members in work, decision making, and recreation. No less important are the culturally reinforced expectation of long life and good health; cultural mechanisms used in avoidance of stress and lack of intergenerational conflict. All these factors are most conducive to longevity.

The absence of a comprehensive written racial history of the area and the short period in which medical studies have taken place preclude a clear answer to Abkhasian longevity. Genetic selectivity is an obvious possibility. As far as can be determined, the Abkhasians are an autochthonous people, eighty generations having occupied the same land for at least 3000 years—a timespan so long that they must have adapted physically to specific elements in their environment.

Constant hand-to-hand combat during many centuries may have eliminated those with poor eyesight, poor hearing, obesity, and other physical shortcomings which would militate against longevity. Repeatedly, this land has been ravaged by invaders, and the Abkhasians themselves have gone on bloody pillages against neighboring tribes. In order to defend themselves against surprise raids, in which many individuals and whole families were carried off into slavery, the Abkhasians could not permit themselves to become exhausted by frequent childbirth, orgiastic sex, excessive drinking, or overeating. Both men and women were required to ride on horseback and shoot well, and to be agile and slender. Only the strongest stock survived those devastating eras.

Physical fitness is still an important requirement. The villagers are not charitable in evaluating the physical attributes of prospective marriage partners. While those with congenital defects are not ruthlessly excluded or maintained in custodial isolation, they, however, are prevented from marrying and thereby from becoming a part of the breeding population. Illegitimacy is deeply condemned, and, unlike in other cultures, a woman considered unfit for marriage by virtue of a physical defect would have no chance to produce offspring.

Aside from inheritance, proper diet, and sufficient exercise, there is another broader aspect of their culture which is of primary importance in maintaining

Nadezhda Bartsis, from the village of Blabyrkha, born 1860. Except for a tooth-ache in her seventies, she claims she has never been ill.

long life and good health. The high degree of integration and continuity in their personal and national lives permits the Abkhasians as a people to adapt themselves —yet preserve themselves—to the changing conditions of the larger society of which they are now a part.

At any given time, their kinship system integrates the different socioeconomic groups, providing them with common values and standards of behavior. At present, and even more so in former times, every individual undergoes similar experiences sequentially, according to age and sex. To be sure, during the feudal period, class distinctions determined the amount of work one performed, but class did not influence the amount of respect due one for age or family position. In addition, the custom of sending one's child to be brought up by a family of lower social class, and incorporating that family into one's own by ritual adoption, ensured that all Abkhasians would be raised in the same manner. As a result, the behavior of people, in daily life and on special occasions as well, is highly formalized and predictable.

The consanguineal and affinal relationships that make up the foundation of this kinship structure, supplemented by a variety of ritual relationships, serves to broaden the human environment from which Abkhasians derive their extraordinary

Teba Sharmat, 115 years old, from the village of Dzherda.

sense of personal identity. These relationships involve lifetime obligations and give each individual an unshaken feeling of security and continuity.

Another factor which serves to integrate the generations in Abkhasia is the kinship terminology, which does not make a distinction between generations. For example, a man uses the term aeshcha for his brothers and all men who carry his family name, except his parents, grandparents, sons, and grandsons. That is, all men who are members of his lineage are his brothers, regardless of generation; whereas English terminology would distinguish among them as nephews, cousins of first and second degrees, grand-nephews and so on. The oldest still command the most respect, generally; but in those cases where a man's uncle is younger than he is, he is still quite deferential to the uncle. A man's friends are generally his age-mates, but loyalty to the lineage overrides any other consideration.

The lack of competition reduces stress and eliminates the fear of failure. According to the rules of kinship, one's status increases with age relative to other members of the family, and does not depend on wealth or occupation. An old person is respected simply by virtue of being old, and is not required to compete with younger people on their terms.

The temporal integration of Abkhasians is expressed in its generational continuity, in the absence of limiting, defining conditions of existence, like "adolescent," "alienated," or "retired." Transition from one age group to another is not marked, and familistic social structures are not replaced by youth groups. There are no sharp discontinuities between the activities, diet, and life styles of the younger and older people. The children and young people participate in all family functions and other aspects of life, like sickness and death. Children are not taught things which are considered "nice" for a certain age, but which the grown-ups obviously

Shkhangeri Bzhania, who was 148 years old at the time this picture was taken. He was noted as a storyteller with a great memory.

do not believe. The shared knowledge and common standards of ethics and morality make for the greatest bond between generations. Abkhasians see life as proceeding on an even keel from cradle to grave with gradual assumption of responsibilities and lack of sudden transitions.

The solid basis of the Abkhasian family is built on the noncompetitive, fully complementary, well-defined patterns of duties and authority in which several generations are bound to each other. Its strength lies in the solidarity and stability of the family as an operating unit.

From the time an Abkhasian is born until he dies, generations later, he leads an orderly, structured life marked by continuity in patterns of work, diet, and social life.

Gradual change, consistency in behavior and the development of a stoic life style from earliest childhood have prepared Abkhasians for the stresses of poverty, warfare, and natural accidents without subjecting them to unnecessary emotional or physical trauma. This seems to coincide with Pavlov's view that early aging is caused by constant overtaxing of the nervous system. He felt that the strengthening and sparing use of the central nervous system plays the most important role in longevity.[1] The Abkhasians can take severe blows without going to pieces, and they have developed a peculiar optimism, in spite of centuries of economic hardship and uncertain living conditions.

The Abkhasians are respectful of their bodies and the bodies of others. They do not physically punish either adults or children (or even animals), and their code of behavior requires that a man show respect to the dead body of his enemy as well. They are also respectful of the privacy and physical autonomy of their children, which partially accounts for the lack of resentment between generations.

Social deprivation following retirement and poor living conditions are common among the single elderly in many industrial societies. In the total area of the Soviet Union, people aged sixty and over and who live alone constitute 10.5 percent of the elderly population. According to Soviet gerontologists, these elderly suffer from "loneliness." This state of loneliness and dissatisfaction with their lot often results in steady deterioration of physical and mental abilities. Often loneliness, to a certain extent, reflects general tendencies for families to be separated into generations.

The Abkhasian, on the other hand, shows a different picture—one of wide participation of the aged in family and social activities. They are never excluded because they belong to a "different generation," but are given the same love, respect, and authority they have always enjoyed.

The inclusion of the most aged in family matters acts as an outlet for their energy, provides a way of self-expression, and satisfies their desire to be needed and important.

Aged Abkhasians are strongly motivated to maintain communication with other people by receiving guests, visiting relatives and friends, watching horse races, and participating in the village councils. For their knowledge and experience are

---

[1] I. P. Pavlov, *Lectures in Physiology*. Moscow: Academy of Science of the USSR, 1952, pp. 351–352.

not outdated, but have the same relevance for the younger generation as for the older.

The Abkhasians may appear rigid to some, but I consider them flexible, a people who bend to the demands of life without surrendering. For centuries they have shown extraordinary adaptability to ecological, economic, political, and religious pressures, maintaining at the same time the core of their culture intact. The people are selective about cultural change. They accept what can be successfully integrated into their society, and are slow to make any changes which would impinge on their traditions. They are unusual, however, in that they adapt to change before it is required of them. Under the Soviet government, Abkhasians have again demonstrated their positive attitude toward reality.

All travelers and foreign visitors have remarked about the Abkhasian feeling of self-esteem and, at the same time, their respect for other people. The Abkhasians are quite confident of themselves. They feel that they are strong, both physically and mentally. Their difficult language gives them an additional sense of unity and uniqueness, and enhances their desire to preserve their culture. Invariably, the first and last toast at an Abkhasian banquet is: "Long live Abkhasia."

The Abkhasians have not yet discovered the fountain of youth. But they have developed what I believe is the next best thing—youthful old age.

Glossary

ab: Father.

abdu: Grandfather; literally, big father.

abipara: Group of relatives, subdivision of an *aeshara*. The word means "sons of one father" and its members trace their ancestry to a single progenitor.

abista: Cornmeal mush, the Abkhasian staple food.

Adats: Caucasian customary laws.

adzhika: A sharp sauce made from red pepper and other spices.

aenshcha: Mother's brother; literally, "mother's blood."

aeshara: Group of relatives, subdivision of an *azhvala*. The word means "brotherhood" or "fraternity."

aeshcha: Brother (from *ashcha*, blood).

agara: A quest or expedition in search of honor.

aila aikhaba: Chief of the council of a lineage.

a-indu: The extended family, subdivision of an abipara. Also, the house in which one's parents live. The word literally means "big house."

Akh: In feudal times, the prince of all Abkhasia.

akh'm: Head, chieftain.

akh'mz: Heroic deeds.

akh'mdyzg: Disgrace.

akhupkha: A child of one family, raised by another, in order to cement ties between the two families.

akyta: Land belonging to an abipara.

alicha: Fruit grown in the Caucasus.

amash-shar: Forbidden day, on which members of a lineage may not do certain types of work.

amhara: Straw hut, used by teenage girls if the house is not large enough to provide them with rooms of their own. Also used by newlyweds for a few weeks after marriage, and by mothers after childbirth.

an: Mother.

anshan: Suit of clothes displayed on a man's bed for a month after his death.

apkhartsa: Musical instrument resembling a dulcimer.

Apsni: Abkhasians' name for their country.

Apsua: Abkhasians' name for themselves. The word means "the people" or "the souls."

ascha: Blood.

ataatzva: Three or four generation family, subdivision of a-indu.

atalyk: A Turkic word denoting a relationship in which one family raises the child of another family in order to establish kinship relationships between them. In Soviet ethnographic literature, the word used is *atalychestvo*. The Abkhasians' name for this custom is *akhashvara*.

Atzan: Member of a legendary race of dwarfs.

atzuta: Territory of a lineage.

Avnadara: Adoption of a child or adult (except for atalyk).

azara: A man who raises another's child (in atalyk).

azhvala: The lineage, whose members have the same surname.

-Ba, -Pa: Suffixes meaning "son." *-ipa* means "his son."

bashlick: Traditional Abkhasian headdress for males.

burka: A long sleeveless felt cape.

cherkesska: A man's belted tunic, common to all Caucasian peoples, with long sleeves, descending to mid-calf and bearing a row of cartridge pouches on the chest.

daddu: Great-great-grandfather.

khachapuri: Cheese-filled pastry, baked without sugar, and eaten on festive occasions.

kalym: Bride price given by the groom, and in Abkhasia, used by the woman's family to purchase her dowry. The term is common through the Caucasus and Central Asia.

kelekhi-ainykhra: Traditional, highly elaborate Abkhasian funeral.

kepi: Headdress worn by Abkhasian males.

kiaraz: The custom of mutual help in agriculture.

matzoni: Buttermilk.

mullah: A Moslem religious functionary.

Nart: Member of a legendary race of heroes.

Shiriat: Islamic law.

Tamada: Elected host at a banquet, who sees to it that toasts are conducted in proper order.

Uraza (Ramadan): The ninth month of the year, a period of daily fasting from sunrise to sunset in Moslem countries.

Bibliography

With the exception of the works by L. J. Luzbetak, W. C. McKain, S. Rosen *et al.*, I. P. Pavlov, and N. N. Sachuk, all of the books and articles cited are available only in Russian, Abkhasian, or Georgian.

BOOKS

Adzhindzhal, I. A. A., *Ethnography of Abkhasia.* Sukhumi: Alashara, 1969.

Akaba, L. Kh., *The Sources of the Religion of the Abkhasians.* Tbilisi: Metzniereba, 1970.

Anshba, A. A., *The Poetics of the Abkhasian Narts Epic.* Tbilisi: Metzniereba, 1970.

Aristav, Sh. K., *et al., The Grammar of the Abkhasian Language.* Sukhumi: Alashara, 1968.

Brazhba, Kh. S., *Abkhasian Fairy Tales.* Sukhumi: Alashara, 1965.

Bzhaniya, Ts. N., "Family and Family Life in an Abkhasian Collective Village," in L. Kh. Akaba and Sh. D. Inal-Ipa (eds.), *The Contemporary Abkhasian Village.* Tbilisi: Metzniereba, 1967.

Daraseliya, I. N., "A Study of the Distribution of Coronary Arteriosclerosis and Its Relation to Diet," in *Anthology of Papers by Physicians of Ostroumov Republican Hospital in Sukhumi.* Sukhumi: Alashara, 1965.

Dzidzaria, G. A., *History of the Abkhasian ASSR.* Sukhumi: Alashara, 1960.

Guseinzade, G., *Azerbaijan: Land of Long-Living People.* Baku: Azerbaijan State Publishers, 1971.

Inal-Ipa, Sh. D., *Abkhasia.* Sukhumi: Alashara, 1965.

————, *Pages of Abkhasian Historical Ethnography.* Sukhumi: Alashara, 1971.

————, "The Social Function of *Atalyk* Relationships in Nineteenth-Century Abkhasia," in *Works of the Abkhasian Institute of Language, Literature, and History,* vol. XXV. Sukhumi: Alashara, 1955.

————, *Studies in the History of Marriage and the Family in Abkhasia.* Sukhumi: Avgiz, 1954.

Kakiashvili, D. C., in *Transactions of the Scientific Sessions of Practicing Physicians in Sukhumi, 1970,* pp. 145-147. Sukhumi: Alashara, 1970.

Kashba, I. M., "Musical Culture of the Abkhasians," in *The Contemporary Abkhasian Village. . . .*

Khidoya, *Commentary on Moslem Justice,* Vol. 2. Tashkent, 1893.

Kuchberia, L. E., "On the Development of Marriage Customs and Wedding Rites among the Abkhasians," in *The Contemporary Abkhasian Village. . . .*

Luzbetak, L. J., *Marriage and the Family in Caucasia.* Vienna: St. Gabriel's Mission Press, 1951.

Maliya, E. M., *Pictorial Folk Art of Abkhasia,* Tbilisi: Metzniereba, 1970.

Pavlov, I. P., *Lectures in Physiology.* Moscow: Academy of Sciences of the USSR, 1952.

Shafiro, I., Y. Darsania, I. Kortua, and V. Chikvatia, *Longevity in Abkhasia*. Suk-humi: Abkhasian State Publishers, 1956.
Sichinava, G. N., "The Characteristics of the Nervous System and Psychological State of the Aged People of Abkhasia," *Anthology of Papers*. . . .
———, "On the Question of the Character and Range of Work Done by the Aged People of Abkhasia," *Anthology of Papers*. . . .
Smyr, G. V., *Islam in Abkhasia*. Tbilisi: Metzniereba, 1972.
Tarba, I., *The Sun Is Rising for Us*. Moscow: Soviet Writer, 1970. Translated into Russian from the Abkhasian by V. Soloukin.
Zvanba, S. T., *Ethnographic Studies*. Sukhumi: Alashara, 1955.

JOURNALS AND PAPERS

Alikshiev, R. Sh., "Characteristics of Longevity in Daghestan." *Proceedings*, Ninth International Congress on Gerontology, Kiev, 1972.
Avidzba, A., "Let's Wipe Out Obsolete Rituals: Again the Kelekhi-Ainykhra," *Soviet Abkhasia*, June 15, 1970.
Chebotarov, D. F., and N. N. Sachuk, "Long-Living People of the Soviet Union." Laboratory of Demography and Sanitary Statistic Institute of Gerontology, Kiev, 1972.
———, "The Aged in Urbanizing Societies." *Proceedings*. . . .
Gogokhiya, Sh. D., and G. N. Sichinava, "The Older People of Abkhasia, Their Health and Mode of Life." *Proceedings*. . . .
Isazade, H. M., *et al.*, "Some Data on Longevity in Azerbaijan." *Proceedings*. . . .
Kakiashvili and Sadofiev, "Roentgenological Data on the Anatomy and the Func-tion of the Circulatory System in Abkhasia." *Transactions of the Academy of Sciences of the Georgian SSR*, vol. 51, No. 2, 1968.
Kosven, M. O., "The *Atalyk* Relationship." *Soviet Ethnography*, Vol. 2, 1935.
McKain, W. C., "Are They Really That Old? Some Observations Concerning Extreme Old Age in the Soviet Union." *The Gerontologist*, vol. 7, No. 1, 1967.
———, "Visit to a Russian Village," *The Courant Magazine*, April 16, 1967.
———, "The Zone of Health." *The Gerontologist*, vol. 9, No. 1, 1969.
Pitskhelauri, G. Z., and A. S. Agadzhanov, "Some Problems in Connection with the Life Styles of Older and Long-Living People of Georgia." *Proceedings*. . . .
Pitskhelauri, G. Z., and D. A. Dzhorbenadze, "Social Demography of the Long-Living Population of the Georgian SSR." *Proceedings*. . . .
Rosen, S., N. Preobrazhensky, S. Khechinashvili, I. Glazunov, N. Kipshidze and H. V. Rosen. "Epidemiologic Hearing Studies in the USSR." *Archives of Otolaryngology* vol. 91, 1970. pp. 424–428.
Sachuk, N. N., "The Geography of Longevity in the USSR." *Geriatrics*, July 1965, pp. 605–606.
Sichinava, G. N., "Long-Term Observations of the Health of Long-Living People." *Proceedings*. . . .
———, N. N. Sachuk, and Sh. D. Gogokhiya, "On the Physical Condition of the Aged People of the Abkhasian ASSR." *Soviet Medicine*, vol. 5, 1964.
Smirnova, Y. S., "*Atalyk* Customs and Adoption in Nineteenth- and Twentieth-Century Abkhasia," *Soviet Ethnography*, No. 2, 1951, pp. 105–114.
———, "Military Democracy in the Narts Epic." *Soviet Ethnography*, vol. 6, 1959.
Smyr, G. V., *Some Moslem Rituals of the Abkhasians: Restrictions on the Right of Women to Speak*. Unpublished manuscript in the Ethnographic Institute in Sukhumi, 1969.
Sultanov, M. N., "Physical Activity and Nutrition of Longevous People of Azer-baijan SSR." *Proceedings*. . . .